Baseless Hatred

What It Is and
What You Can Do about It

René H. Levy, Phd

gefen publishing house
JERUSALEM • NEW YORK • Est. 1981

Scripture quotations are from The Holy Scriptures According to the Masoretic
Text, published by the Jewish Publication Society in 1917.

Cover Design and Typesetting by Stephanie & Ruti Design

3 5 7 9 8 6 4 2 1

Gefen Publishing House Ltd.

6 Hatzvi Street, Jerusalem 94386, Israel

972-2-538-0247

orders@gefenpublishing.com

Gefen Books

600 Broadway, Lynbrook, NY 11563, USA

1-800-477-5257

orders@gefenpublishing.com

www.gefenpublishing.com

Printed in Israel

Send for our free catalogue

ISBN: 978-965-229-530-9

To my wife, Beloria

This book is the result of her vision and guidance

About the Author

René H. Levy holds a BS in Pharmacy from the University of Paris and a PhD in Pharmaceutical Chemistry from the University of California, San Francisco. He is Professor Emeritus of Pharmaceutics at the University of Washington School of Pharmacy, where he founded the department of pharmaceutics and served as its chair for twenty-six years. Prof. Levy was a faculty member of the department of neurological surgery for more than thirty-five years. He has published hundreds of research articles, mainly in neuropharmacology, and co-edited several books, including Metabolic Drug Interactions and Antiepileptic Drugs. The author has been named Fellow of the American Association for the Advancement of Science, and recently received a lifetime achievement award for his work on the treatment of epilepsy. He is married with three children and lives in Seattle.

Contents

Preface

Why would a laboratory scientist write on the topic of hatred? Why shift from forty-five years of "hard science" to what is at best "soft science"?[1]

It had little to do with science. I was "drafted" to take on this endeavor a couple of years ago, through an unexpected set of circumstances. I had just given a public lecture and as I was leaving, I was approached by a young rabbi who introduced himself and very politely asked whether I would be willing to prepare a lecture on the topic of "baseless hatred," and to deliver it in his community. The young man knew that he was making an odd request, but his poise and earnestness provided much of the missing context. I responded politely that although the linkage between neuropharmacology and baseless hatred is distant, I would take his request under consideration.

Out of curiosity, I conducted a rapid literature search on the topic of baseless hatred, expecting to find numerous books that would provide background material for one lecture. To my surprise, I could not even find an explicit definition of the association of words baseless hatred. That felt strange, since it is common knowledge that baseless hatred has been associated with the longest exile of the Jewish people from the Land of Israel. I became particularly intrigued by the difference, if any, between "common" or "generic" hatred and the Jewish concept of "baseless" or "causeless" hatred. I examined the literature on generic hatred and was even more surprised to find that, even among experts, there was not an agreed-upon definition of the basic human emotion of hatred.

---

1   This differentiation between" hard" and "soft" science is borrowed from the eminent neuropsychologist Chris Frith, *Making Up the Mind: How the Brain Creates Our Mental World* (Malden, MA: Blackwell Publishing, 2007), 3–9.

At that point, my scientific curiosity took over; I researched the topic and eventually prepared a fifty-minute presentation. That lecture included a description of the characteristics of hatred based on psychology and neurobiology as well as a differentiation between hatred and baseless hatred. I proposed that baseless hatred is a Jewish concept because hatred destroys the cement that has kept the Jewish people united as a nation, even when it did not live on its land: that cement is called *arevut*, which means "mutual responsibility." The lecture also showed that baseless hatred behaves as a sort of contagious disease that destroys interpersonal relationships whether in the family, among friends, or in the workplace. Most importantly, it dissolves away the unity of the Jewish people and they lose their "title" to the Land of Israel.

The reaction to the lecture was overwhelming: somehow, it seemed that the topic had hit a sensitive nerve in several audiences. CDs and DVDs of the lecture were prepared and they quickly ran out. My wife, who had witnessed the reactions of various audiences, decided that I had a responsibility to write the lecture material in a formal fashion.

As soon as I began, it became evident that, in spite of the success of the initial lecture, its focus had been narrow because it had been aimed at Orthodox Jews living in the Diaspora. In reality, baseless hatred represents a challenge for the Jewish people as a whole, obviously including Israeli Jews. Jews in Israel constitute the first autonomous Jewish society built in nineteen centuries, and they confront the issue of baseless hatred on a daily basis and on multiple levels – socioeconomic, religious, and political. Furthermore, the very existence of the State of Israel raises a unique question. Since baseless hatred and exile from the Land of Israel have been connected in a historical paradigm throughout Jewish history, we must ask: Does the paradigm work in reverse? Did the return of the Jews to their land in 1948 spell the end of baseless hatred among Jews?

To address the nature and status of baseless hatred in Israel, it became necessary to examine the impact on Israeli society of external factors such as the Islamist anti-Zionist hostility and the more recent Western antisemitic opposition (see chapters 5 through 7). I felt that an understanding of the underpinnings of this global external hatred confronting Israel would minimize the tendency to turn it into a divisive wedge within Israeli society; also, it would help provide answers to the new existential questions posed by the post-Zionist movement.

Another consequence of this understanding is the proposal to initiate a global *arevut* or mutual responsibility program including Israel and the Diaspora (chapter 8). Baseless hatred can be fought and overcome at the individual level if it is acknowledged as a lethal disease that causes pain and anguish within Jewish families. Like other hidden diseases, it can be conquered if it is brought out in the open and addressed formally in the curricula of Jewish schools. The book's last two chapters (9 and 10) provide detailed, step-by-step approaches for the prevention of new episodes and the repair of existing episodes of baseless hatred.

At present, hatred has become a worldwide global issue because it causes wars and genocides. It is my hope that this analysis of baseless hatred, which focuses on the long struggle of one people with the human emotion of hatred, might also be of interest to the broader, non-Jewish public. It is submitted to all with the utmost humility.

Acknowledgments

First of all, I wish to thank God, who guided and sustained us during this endeavor.

I am grateful to Rabbi Solomon Maimon, my teacher and mentor for the last forty years, for his encouragement to take on this task, for helpful discussions during the writing, and for his support of the end product. I am also thankful to Rabbi Simon Benzaquen and to Rabbi Haim Gourdji for their trust and support since the onset of the project.

I am indebted to several individuals who reviewed early versions of the manuscript: Ms. Judy Lash Balint, Ms. Lynne Behar, and my brother, Mr. Francois Levy. I wish to thank our friends, Mr. and Mrs. Eli and Rebecca Almo and Mr. and Mrs. Larry and Fortun Azose, for their passion in addressing the challenges posed by baseless hatred. In the same vein, I acknowledge Ms. Vivian Uria for her determination and all-out dedication to spread the "*arevut* message" within Israeli society.

I am profoundly grateful to my family, who provided emotional support from the outset of the project and throughout its gestation. First and foremost is my wife, Mrs. Beloria Levy, who read multiple drafts of the manuscript and has been a partner every step of the way, providing vision, love, inspiration, support, and trust. I am deeply indebted to my holy parents, Joseph and Madeleine Levy, of blessed memory, for providing me with the most precious set of caring and supportive siblings: Dr. Samuel Levy, for numerous insightful discussions on the fundamental messages of Judaism and the uniqueness of our people; Ms. Liliane Shalom, who personifies the trait of empathy and who toiled for months to enhance the message and success of this book; Mr. Francois Levy, for putting his sharp and analytical mind to review two drafts of the manuscript under tight deadlines and making key suggestions; and Dr. Maurice Levy, Ms. Rita Czech, and Ms. Marilyn Levy, for their encouragement and support of this project when it was in its infancy.

To my children, Dr. and Mrs. Elie and Miriam Levy, Drs. Eli and Orlie Cohen, and Dr. Daniel Levy: words cannot convey the significance of your encouragement, respect, love, and support throughout the phases of this endeavor.

I owe special thanks to the exceptional staff of Gefen Publishing House in Jerusalem: Mr. Ilan Greenfield and Mr. Michael Fischberger, for their impeccable leadership; Ms. Kezia Raffel Pride, for her diligent copy-editing work, filtering ideas and providing suggestions; and Ms. Smadar Belilty, for her professional and enthusiastic assistance during the production phase.

Introduction

Baseless Hatred: A Subject of Jewish Interest

For centuries, the concept of hatred[1] has fascinated psychologists, philosophers, and scientists, such as Aristotle, Descartes, Darwin, and Freud. Hatred is part of the spectrum of normal human emotions, but it is particularly difficult to define. Hatred is associated with negative connotations, yet it is meant to serve useful functions, such as helping us avoid threats to our survival. For example, we understand the purpose of hate that allows us to recognize an enemy or to fight a war. But do we understand hate in our immediate environment, among neighbors, in schools, or in the workplace?

When a strong disagreement erupts between close family members and they later hate each other for years, are they using the same hate mechanisms that operate between ethnic groups that commit genocides? Such broad and fundamental questions about hate have been asked by various experts in the field of hate research: "What is hate? Why does it so often lead to the most extreme forms of violence and cruelty? How can hate be stopped?"[2] or "Why is there so much of it? How does it originate, and what can we do about it?"[3]

This book is about hate but its focus is narrower. We are interested in one type of hate that has been labeled "baseless" or "senseless" or "gratuitous" or "causeless." These multiple appellations are needed

---

1   The words hate and hatred are used interchangeably throughout this book.

2   Rush W. Dozier Jr., *Why We Hate: Understanding, Curbing, and Eliminating Hate in Ourselves and Our World* (New York: McGraw-Hill, 2002), cover.

3   Robert J. Sternberg and Karin Sternberg, *The Nature of Hate* (New York: Cambridge University Press, 2008), cover.

because they represent approximate renditions by English authors of the original Hebrew expression *sinat hinam*, which means literally "hatred for free." All of these expressions attempt to convey that somehow there exists a type of hatred that has no basis or that has no logical relationship with its apparent cause.

The original concept of baseless hatred was introduced long ago by the sages of the Talmud in a context that gave it enormous historical significance: namely, the end of the last Jewish Commonwealth in the year 70 of the Common Era.[4] The sages were searching for reasons to explain cataclysmic events that seemed to spell the end of a civilization: the destruction of the Second Temple and of Jerusalem and the exile of the Jewish people from the Land of Israel. Their answer was most surprising: they attributed these catastrophes to the prevalence of baseless hatred among Jews in Israel (Talmud, *Yoma* 9, *Arachin* 15b). The causal link between calamities of historical proportions and a behavior like baseless hatred is not easy to comprehend. How could a whole people be defeated and become homeless just for that reason? It might have been easier to understand if the sages who introduced the notion of baseless hatred had provided us with a definition, but they did not. However, they emphasized its significance as follows:

1. First, they characterized its gravity by pointing out that it is more serious than several other moral failures such as idolatry, immorality, and bloodshed.

2. Then, the sages took it away from the realm of past history and made it relevant to every generation by emphasizing that until baseless hatred disappears, the Temple cannot be rebuilt. That places baseless hatred on the path of Jewish destiny and makes it an issue of permanent concern.

---

4 Some Jewish historians date it instead to the year 68 CE.

3. The sages identified another unique characteristic of baseless hatred when they stated that it existed in the midst of people who practiced Judaism and even performed acts of kindness. This taught something surprising: when it comes to baseless hatred, there is apparently no religious-secular divide. Parenthetically, this last teaching by the sages reflects a high capacity for self-evaluation and a dedication to the search for truth, however uncomfortable.

These dimensions do not explain the nature of baseless hatred and in fact add to the mystery surrounding that concept. Since then, baseless hatred has remained unexplained. Does baseless hatred imply that Jews more than any other people are capable of hating arbitrarily, for no reason? That does not seem correct because we know that in the eyes of a hater, hate always has some justification; it does not erupt randomly. Alternatively, we could consider that hate comes in two forms, one "for cause" and another "without basis," perhaps with the understanding that the former is "non-Jewish" while the latter is the "Jewish type." Such a speculation also violates common sense.

Hate is a complex emotion to understand for several reasons. First, it has many faces, forms, and degrees: at times it is hidden and at other times it manifests itself through extreme violence. On occasion, it appears as a temporary reaction, but at others it behaves as a stable emotional pattern or even a natural predisposition. Also, it can erupt in families among individuals who loved each other, leading to the well-known love-hate switch (husband-wife, parent-child, siblings). Another striking feature is its transmissibility: children seem to absorb it easily at home or at school. Hate can be also transmitted by culture, social conditions, and social groups. This ease of transmission explains how militia groups and terrorist organizations can recruit otherwise normal students on campuses; it also explains why whole populations can be galvanized by "trusted" leaders into a hatred frenzy against internal or external groups.

Historically, hate and violence have always been part of radio and television broadcasts. Recently, because of the ease of transmission, the Internet has provided the merchants of hate with unexpected prospects of success.

In spite of the widespread presence of hate in the lives of individuals and in all societies, the status of knowledge and research in this field remains deficient. As pointed out by experts, "the domain of hate remains largely enigmatic and lacking a strong empirical foundation."[5] In a recent book entitled *The Psychology of Hate*, editor Robert J. Sternberg pointed out in the preface: "A survey of some recent introductory social psychology texts revealed love as an index term in all of them but hate as an index term in none of them."[6] The author deplored this imbalance in interest in the emotion of hate among psychologists, especially in view of the genocide of the Nazis in World War II and the other genocides that have followed during the twentieth century and in the last decade.

When the Nobel Peace Prize laureate Elie Wiesel commented on the devastation associated with September 11, 2001, he wrote: "Can it be explained? Yes, by hatred. Hatred is the root of evil everywhere. Racial hatred, ethnic hatred, political hatred, religious hatred. In its name, all seems permitted. For those who glorify hatred, as terrorists do, the end justifies all means, including the most despicable ones."[7] Thus, the topic of hate is odd because on one hand, we are surrounded by it and able to speak about it routinely, while at the same time experts indicate that it is not understood. If so, how will we be able to address the phenomenon of baseless hatred?

---

5   Roy F. Baumeister and David A. Butz, "Roots of Hate, Violence, and Evil," chapter 5 in *The Psychology of Hate*, ed. Robert J. Sternberg (Washington, DC: American Psychological Association, 2005), 87.

6   Ibid., ix.

7   Elie Wiesel, "We Choose Honor," *Parade*, October 28, 2001, 4–5.

We will proceed in several steps. First, we will start with generic hatred and try to combine the main characteristics of hate described by psychologists with those of neurobiologists. We will learn about the triggers and the manifestations of hate: its relationship to fear and anger, its thousand faces, its rational and irrational aspects. We will discover that hate is triggered because our primitive neural system reacts to events from the perspective of our own preexisting insecurities, because we make generalizations (which may be positive or negative) and confuse associations (additional but not necessarily relevant information) with causality. We will see that once hate has been triggered, it is difficult to extinguish. We will understand the rapid switch that occurs when a person who initially feels victimized turns into a vindictive perpetrator of hate.

In a second phase, we will turn to the topic of hatred among Jews to determine whether it has any specificity. Do Jews hate differently or are they like everyone else? Here, we encounter a few surprises. We learn that Jewish tradition has a deep interest in and appreciation of the human emotion of hatred. Jews encountered the destructive aspects of hatred very early in their history before they ever became a people. From its embryonic stage, the Jewish people experienced a direct relationship between hatred and exile, a relationship that continues until today.

Early on, the forebears of the Jewish people struggled with hatred, its consequences, and its solutions. Out of that struggle emerged the concept of mutual responsibility which I have dubbed "the Judah principle," after its originator (in Hebrew it is called *arevut*). It refers to a commitment to mutual responsibility that must characterize all relationships between Jews. It can be viewed as a "cement" uniting Jews at all times and in all places. Jewish tradition has always had an attitude of zero tolerance of hatred and considers that the various triggers of hatred are invalid – that is, they do not constitute valid reasons for hating – because they originate from character deficiencies such as envy, competition, and jealousy.

When we tally all of these factors, we begin to uncover the characteristics that make hatred among Jews baseless: it is an unfair response that is also avoidable; when it erupts, it lasts and spreads among people and therefore bears no relationship to its original trigger. The reason why baseless hatred is given enormous significance is that it is lethal to the people as a whole: hatred destroys empathy and therefore destroys the invisible link that binds Jews to form the Jewish people. The cement that binds Jews together dissolves and the people is transformed into a group of individuals. The image is that of a building that turns into a pile of bricks because its cement was washed away.

We can crystallize all these features into one definition: baseless hatred is an unfair, excessive, and avoidable reaction by one Jew that transforms another Jew into an enemy and thereby destroys the integrity of the Jewish people.

This navigation through various facets of the history of hatred among Jews and the implications of the above definition make it compelling to address the creation of the State of Israel. For the first time since the long exile triggered by baseless hatred had begun 1,878 years before, the Jewish people had an independent government in its land. Did the return of the Jewish people to the Land of Israel spell the end of baseless hatred among Jews? What has happened to baseless hatred in the last sixty-two years? An analysis of key events in the life of Israel through the lens of baseless hatred reveals an intricate relationship between internal baseless hatred and the external anti-Zionist opposition or hatred. In Israel, the type and extent of external opposition – that is, the Islamist and Western-based hostility faced by Israel, whether it is politically or religiously motivated – has profound repercussions on divisiveness among Jews and on the manifestations of baseless hatred.

Based on these analyses, we arrive at a proposal that the time has come for Israeli and Diaspora Jews to combat baseless hatred through a personal rededication to the old Judah principle. The last two chapters provide a step-by-step approach that individuals can use to prevent new episodes of baseless hatred and to repair existing ones. This analysis shows that all along, the Jews have had a close interface with the human emotion of hatred. It is at the core of their peoplehood, their survival, and their relationship with their land. Baseless hatred remains a challenge to be overcome.

Part 1

Hatred and Its Antidote

1

Generic Hatred

There is no definition of hatred that is both concise and complete. Therefore, a typical starting point in the literature on hate is to cite various definitions that focus on different characteristics. For example, Merriam-Webster's Collegiate Dictionary (11th ed., 2004) defines hate as "intense hostility and aversion usually deriving from fear, anger, or sense of injury." This definition brings up the emotions of fear or anger as starting points but it does not address the sources or causes of fear or anger. As to injury, whether physical or psychological, we know that it does not always result in hate (consider, for example, injury caused by a tornado). This definition does not address the aspect of duration or reversibility of these hostile feelings. Sternberg and Sternberg[1] cite the Webster's New World College Dictionary definition: to hate is "to have strong dislike or ill will for; loathe; despise" and "to dislike or

---

1 Sternberg and Sternberg, *The Nature of Hate*, 16.

wish to avoid; shrink from." One obvious limitation of this definition is that haters tend to pursue and attack the objects of hate, not just avoid them.

In this chapter, we will address the notion of generic hatred borrowing from research in the fields of psychology and neurobiology. Clarity is essential in analyzing the characteristics of hate. In the discussion to follow, we will consider hate that involves two parties: the person who harbors hate is called hater or perpetrator while the other person, the target, is called the victim or object of hate.

Contributions of Psychology

The concept of hatred has fascinated psychologists for centuries. As indicated in the introduction, prominent philosophers and scientists such as Aristotle, Descartes, Darwin, and Freud have all attempted to develop a concise definition of hatred, but with limited success.

Aristotle proposed that hate has three dimensions: it is painless, incurable by time, and makes the hater strive for the annihilation of the object of hate. For Descartes, hate makes the hater withdraw from the object of hate. The contrast between these two perspectives is interesting: Aristotle sees the hater as an aggressor while Descartes sees him as withdrawing. Darwin focuses on a different aspect altogether: for him, hate is a unique feeling because it has no facial sign while it leads to rage toward the object.

Modern psychologists shed additional light on the cause of hate, describing it as an emotion caused by a judgment that the object of hate is evil. In that way, it is different from contempt, since the latter results from a judgment that the object of contempt is inferior. Others disagree and see contempt as a form of "cool hate"[2] since the hater can evolve easily from seeing the object as inferior to being convinced that he is objectively evil. Contempt is a first step toward devaluation; it is part of the type of prejudice that constitutes the seeds of hate. In full-fledged hate, the hater exhibits more than disdain or dislike. The hater becomes obsessed by the object of hate and wishes its destruction.

Relationship of Hate to Anger and Fear

Because hatred is closely related to other emotions such as anger, fear, and love, we need to compare and contrast hate with these emotions.

Fear itself is classified as a fight-or-flight response, with emphasis on flight, meaning that the first instinctive reaction of a frightened person is to run away. If that is impossible, the fearful person will resort to appeasing the opponent; it is only as a last resort that the fearful person decides to fight. For example, when a person is confronted with an armed burglar, the first instinct would be to run to safety. The last resort would be to try to disarm the burglar. The same applies to a mouse when it is caught by a cat: it tries first to escape and only fights as the last resort. Anger is different in that it is also a fight-or-flight response, but with emphasis on fight. The angry person does not run away; he or she is ready to fight and may strike at the object of anger even before realizing what was done.

It turns out that hate includes both anger and fear, both running away and fighting, but in a complex way. Hate can be expressed according to a wide spectrum ranging from anger and rage at one end to avoidance and absolute silence at the other. In addition to anger or silence, other ways of expressing hatred include contempt, even laughter or mockery. For

2   In the expression "cool hate," cool means "cold" as in "ice cold," not "cool" as in "hip" or "fun."

example, a hater would prefer to respond aggressively (with anger) but if that is not possible for logistical or social reasons, the hater hides his feelings (flight reaction). But that lack of reaction is only apparent and temporary; the hate is stored until the hater can respond or take revenge. The strategy of hate is to use avoidance only as a necessary delay of the urge to attack, the goal being the destruction of the object of hate.

We can understand the relationship between hate and fear by observing the reactions that some individuals have to animals or insects like cockroaches or spiders:[3] the person who fears spiders will avoid them and when faced with them will try to have someone else remove them. On the other hand, the person who hates spiders does not really fear them; when faced with them, that person will search them out and try to kill them without hesitation. Thus, hate includes some of the negative feelings toward spiders of the person who fears as well as the aggression of the angry person.

There is another fundamental distinction between hate and anger: duration. Anger is transient; it erupts at a particular time and disappears, and its time course is predictable. Hate, on the other hand, lasts in a way that is sometimes described as a phobia. It is ingrained and becomes like a stored allergic response.

Hatred Is Not Irrational

It is important to note that while hatred may seem irrational because it provokes conflicting actions such as withdrawal and attack, it actually involves selection and discrimination. For example, hatred is not a systematic reaction to harm or injury: we do not typically hate a storm or tornado, even though it may cause us much damage, simply because we do not perceive it as a conscious being responsible for its actions.

---

3 Dozier, *Why We Hate*, 19.

The same applies to young children: in general they are not the target of hatred because we do not perceive them as rational agents responsible for their actions.

The role of reason and rational thinking in the genesis of hatred is illustrated by the fact that young children are not capable of hate because they do not have the cognitive capacity or the maturity necessary to see others as morally responsible. Children can react with much anger, but that is not hatred. Later on, as they mature, they develop the ability to hate (see epilogue). Thus, hatred involves some discrimination when it chooses its target.

Hatred and Love: The Thousand Faces of Hatred

Robert and Karin Sternberg have introduced the duplex theory, which explains why sometimes love turns rapidly into hate (as between husband and wife).[4] In this theory, hate is very closely related to love. They propose that both love and hate have three components that are interrelated. The three components of love are intimacy, passion, and decision/commitment. Likewise the three components of hate are negation of intimacy (manifested by distancing, repulsion, or disgust), passion (manifested in emotions such as anger and/or fear), and decision/commitment (manifested as devaluation/diminution through contempt).

An interesting consequence of this approach to hatred is that various combinations of the three components of hate can explain the different "faces" of hatred. For example the Sternbergs list seven types of hate: cool, hot, cold, boiling, simmering, seething, and burning hate. These different types can all be explained using one or more of the three components. As an example, we will cover three different types: cool, hot, and burning.

---

4 Sternberg and Sternberg, *The Nature of Hate*, 51.

1. Cool hate includes only one component: negation of intimacy. The hater experiences only feelings of disgust and wants nothing to do with the target of hate. The hater seeks distance from the object of hate and avoids interactions with that person. We see that type of behavior quite often after an unpleasant verbal interaction between two individuals. It is not an extreme form of hate but it can last for some time.

2. Hot hate is at the other end of the spectrum because it includes only the one component of passion. The person in the grip of hot hate experiences feelings of anger or fear and reacts either by running away (flight) or by attacking (fight). We see this type sometimes in family fights where one member runs away from the house. We also see it in work-related incidents where the disgruntled employee suddenly quits the workplace and comes back later causing some violence.

3. Burning hate includes all three components: disgust with anger/fear and with devaluation/diminution. This hate is the most extreme form and is associated with a need on the part of the hater to destroy the target of hate. In this case the hater is trapped by the hate until he obtains revenge. That is the type of hate associated with political, ethnic, and religious conflicts that include violent behavior. The Sternbergs point out that an interesting aspect of this theory is that these different types of hate are not absolute and can overlap, yielding even more combinations, thus explaining why hatred can have a thousand faces.

For our purposes, we can summarize these psychological characterizations of hatred as follows: hatred is essentially a response, a reaction to some past event perceived as injurious; it does not emerge in a vacuum or in the absence of a preceding interaction with a person (even if the interaction is through a third party); when the hater shares his or her feelings, they are of the type "I was treated unfairly! I was abused for no reason!" Thus, the hater justifies his hate feelings by considering himself a victim.

Strangely enough, hatred can also emerge as a response to an anticipated injury that may or may not be real; all that counts is the perception or the belief that it might take place sometime in the future. This belief is sufficient to generate hatred, even if it is not founded. Even when it is not visible, hate has consequences: the attitude of the hater is vindictive or vengeful. At a minimum, the attitude is unfriendly or antagonistic; generally, the hater feels an urge to eliminate or even destroy the object of hate. The feeling of hate tends to last and is considered a stable emotional pattern. Hate has staying power and does not just disappear after an incident. According to some authors, it can even be incurable.

Contributions of Neurobiology

A few notions from neurobiology are helpful to understand some of the mechanics and manifestations of hate.[5] Anatomical and functional pathways of human emotions are complex subjects beyond the scope of our analysis. One simplified but useful notion used in the field of hatred has been to schematically divide our neural system into two components: the primitive neural system (associated with the inner part of the brain) and the advanced neural system (associated with the cerebral cortex). In the primitive neural system, one organ of interest, the amygdala, is responsible for several emotions and motivations – particularly hate, anger, fear, joy, and love – and functions to promote our survival through

---

5   Dozier, *Why We Hate*, 17, 57, 65.

its connections to the sensory systems.[6] Information received by our senses is scanned and rapidly evaluated for any sign of threat or pain. If one is perceived, it triggers a response even before we are able to realize what is happening. Examples include ducking, jumping, or screaming at the sight of a danger or threat; these are called preconscious responses.

This "guardian" role of the amygdala is visible in animals with natural enemies (mice and cats or cats and dogs) because they lose their aggressive behaviors when their amygdalae are removed. A useful summary image of the primitive neural system is that of a reptile: it has been called "the reptile within" because reptiles feel only pain and pleasure, they operate from instinct, are territorial, and are not social (they do not bond and usually do not care for their young).

The advanced neural system is responsible for our most advanced abilities (self-awareness and consciousness) and is capable of sophisticated functions such as interpretation, conceptualization, and providing meaning. It allows us to reflect, contemplate, and have foresight. Of particular significance here, it is responsible for our capacity of empathy, of feeling for others.[7] The primitive and advanced neural systems communicate and tend to compete for the control of our thoughts, emotions, and behavior as follows: the amygdala stores the information it receives from the sensory systems and classifies it in a primitive way (positive, negative) that is difficult to alter. On the other hand, the emotional judgments and evaluations made by the

---

6 R.J. Dolan, "The Human Amygdala and Orbital Prefrontal Cortex in Behavioural Regulation," in *Mental Processes in the Human Brain*, ed. Jon Driver et al. (New York: Oxford University Press, 2008), 49–68; Frith, *Making Up the Mind*, 46–47, 177–78.

7 Marcello Spinella, "Prefrontal Substrates of Empathy: Psychometric Evidence in a Community Sample," *Biological Psychiatry* 70, no. 3 (December 2005): 175–81; Frith, *Making Up the Mind*, 149–50.

advanced neural system are more abstract, capable of being altered as new information becomes available and thus more open to reasoning.

Hate and the Primitive Neural System

Hate is associated with our primitive neural system because it is programmed to help us avoid threats to our survival. This association is essential to an understanding of the nature of hatred. The primitive neural system has four characteristics relevant to hatred.

1. The primitive neural system dictates responses based on our own insecurities. Due to our insecurities, small triggers such as a criticism, a joke, or even a facial expression can trigger a hatred response because they are perceived (often misinterpreted) as a form of aggression. The recipient feels attacked and trapped, and unleashes a primitive neural system response. It does not matter whether the criticism was meant to be constructive; the recipient's low threshold of insecurity will cause it to be viewed as an assault.

    ### Scenario 1.1: The Full Plate

    The following scene takes place at a social event where food is served in a buffet style. Reuven helps himself and is returning to join his wife at their table. Shimon sees Reuven's full plate and says to him: "Reuven, you must be hungry!" Reuven, who is obese, does not appreciate this remark and is visibly offended; he just stares back at Shimon without saying anything and returns to his table, muttering to his wife, "Who gives him the right to comment on my plate? Who does he think he is? Ever since his daughter married the rabbi's son, he believes he has the right to judge everyone else!" His wife answers, "No! I think that since they bought their new house, he and his wife think they're better than the rest of us."

This type of overreaction is worthy of analysis. Reuven did not reply at all to Shimon's comment, which was about Reuven being hungry at that time, or, by extension, about the amount of food on the plate. Reuven did not consider for an instant that the comment might be a way of making casual conversation or a friendly joke. Reuven perceived the comment as an attack; he felt embarrassed and questioned Shimon's right to say what he did. This is a clear example of Reuven's primitive neural system reacting due to his own insecurity about eating too much.

2.   The primitive neural system sees causality where there is only association. In scenario 1.1 above, Reuven associated Shimon's comment about his plate with something totally unrelated, his perception of Shimon's new social status as a result of the marriage of his daughter, which is a complete fabrication. Reuven's wife brought in her own resentment of the fact that Shimon bought a new house. These two reactions are clear cases of fabricated or misplaced causality. In addition, his wife's reaction is a case of hatred by association (see chapter 3).

3.   The primitive neural system thinks in broad categories. In scenario 1.1, in Reuven's mind, Shimon was instantly transformed from good to bad, with no shades of gray, no in-betweens. There was no room for giving Shimon the benefit of the doubt, no alternative interpretation, and no discrimination between Shimon's good and bad qualities. Eliminating all these analytical modes is what allows the primitive neural system to enable rapid responses when a person feels threatened. The classic example given in neurobiology is that once a person has been bitten by a snake, the primitive neural system marks the snake as a serious threat to help us avoid future accidents. To be efficient, it does so without discrimination and stores that information indefinitely in its database. Because it thinks only in

broad stereotypes, at the next opportunity the person will react in the same way to any snake, whether or not it is venomous. The rational mind is not able to interfere with that reaction even at a later time.

4. The primitive neural system fixates on the past and is highly resistant to change. Once the neural system has marked something as a threat, the perception of danger endures. Thus, any pain caused by past wrongs remains as vivid as if it had just occurred. The hater never forgets the words that offended him or her, no matter how much time elapses.

Scenario 1.2: The Wedding Dress

This scene took place on the night of the wedding of Sarah to Avi. As Sarah came out in her wedding dress, her mother-in-law (Avi's mother) saw her and made a comment about the length of her dress. Sarah looked back at her in a way that showed that she was offended. Twenty years later, the family organizes a celebration of Sarah's mother-in-law's seventieth birthday. Avi and Sarah are talking at home before going to the party and Avi becomes exasperated: he cannot understand how Sarah is able to recite word for word her mother in-law's comment twenty years earlier, when in their daily life, Sarah often misplaces keys and forgets passwords and appointments.

Avi was offended that Sarah had remembered a negative comment. He did not realize that Sarah was not making a special effort of memory to remember the twenty-year-old incident. Her primitive neural system had taken an exact snapshot of all the details surrounding that event and kept it alive at all times, simply because she had interpreted the comment as hurtful.

Similarly, in scenario 1.1, Reuven never forgot Shimon's words and from that day onward, he was distant toward Shimon and avoided speaking to him.

Consequences of the Role of the Primitive Neural System in Hate

Because of its role in survival and reproduction, the primitive neural system functions as a high-alert system that protects our emotional needs, including our vulnerabilities and our inner insecurities. Before responding with hatred, a person first feels threatened and trapped. But once that happens, hatred tends to exhibit a low-threshold trigger: that is, it is easily triggered. This has serious consequences on the two key dimensions of hatred: its emergence and its consequences. On one hand, hatred can emerge very rapidly, even for trivial reasons; on the other, it is long lasting and also transforms the hater into a person who is vindictive and loses empathy for the victim of hate. The result is a disproportionate gap between the causes and consequences of hatred.

Summary

We now understand that generic hatred is a basic human emotion meant to serve useful functions such as helping us avoid threats to our survival. Based on the disciplines of psychology and neurobiology, we derived the following key characteristics: (1) hate is essentially a reaction – usually an overreaction – that occurs when an individual feels threatened or trapped; (2) it has a low threshold and can be triggered by stimuli that are real or imagined; (3) the individual who hates makes generalized judgments and confuses associations with causality, linking irrelevant information to the emergence of hatred; (4) the hater has a vindictive, revengeful attitude toward his target; (5) once hatred develops, it does not disappear; it cannot be simply extinguished.

With this background about generic hatred, we are in a position to address the topic of hatred among Jews, specifically baseless hatred.[8]

---

8 The reader interested only in methods to prevent or repair episodes of hatred can turn to chapters 10 and 11.

2

Hatred among Jews

The characteristics of hatred that we just described are generic and therefore relevant to all humans. In the present chapter, we learn that Jews have had a special awareness of the basic human emotion of hatred. For example, when we analyze how the Jews became a people, we find that they did so through three successive episodes that linked hatred to exile from the Land of Israel (called the land of Canaan at the time). Hatred continued to be a factor in the relationship of the Jewish people with its land throughout its history. In this chapter, we also find out that Jewish tradition has a zero-tolerance attitude toward hatred among Jews and provides a step-by-step methodology to anticipate and prevent the emergence of hatred in interpersonal relationships. All these angles of the relationship between Jews and hatred are covered here as a first phase toward arriving at a definition of the concept of baseless hatred.

Birth in Exile

As the Jews left Egypt in the year 2448 (1312 BCE), they emerged from slavery as a people. Forty years later they entered the land of Canaan. In doing so, they somehow defied a historical law of nation building. Independent of differences among anthropologists and historians about the exact definition of a nation, it stands to reason that any group of like-minded individuals wishing to form a nation can only do so if they first live together in some common territory; whatever other characteristics are shared by those individuals (culture, language, values, physical traits, ethnicity, genetics), shared occupancy of their land or territory is also required for them to evolve into a nation. History shows that a nation cannot come into existence if its citizens are dispersed or nomads with no fixed address. The Jews were an exception to this rule because they were not on their land when they became a people; they were exiled in Egypt. How did that occur? Because of the existence of a pattern of hatred among Jews that lasted several generations. That pattern involved three episodes.

First Hatred-Exile Episode: Hatred of Esau toward Jacob

The first person to be actually born a Hebrew was Isaac, son of Abraham and Sarah.[1] Isaac was born in the land of Canaan and never left it, not even for essential needs such as finding a wife. He and his wife Rebecca had twin sons, Jacob and Esau, who seemed to have different personalities right from the womb. When Isaac became old and wished to bless Esau (who was the firstborn twin, although he abdicated his firstborn status when he sold his birthright to his brother in exchange for a bowl of soup[2]), Rebecca determined (based, in traditional Jewish

---

1   For more details on this episode, consult Genesis 25:19.

2   Genesis 25:31–34.

understanding, on prophecy that she received) that Jacob should receive the blessing instead. She devised a substitution plan and convinced Jacob to go along and obtain the blessing by presenting to his father a meal that his mother had prepared.

The plan succeeded and when Esau found out, he harbored feelings of hatred toward Jacob and expressed the desire to kill him after the death of their father. When Rebecca heard about Esau's plan, she asked Jacob to leave the land of Canaan and join her brother Lavan in Haran. This is how the hatred of Esau forced Jacob to leave the Land of Israel and be exiled. There is evidence (from Jacob's dream) that Jacob was greatly pained to have to go into exile. Indeed, this episode had far-reaching consequences on the life of Jacob (his marriage to Rachel and Leah) and eventually on his children.

Second Hatred-Exile Episode: Hatred of Joseph's Brothers

After twenty years, Jacob returned to the land of Canaan, where his children became shepherds and again experienced tension between siblings.[3] Joseph, the older of the two sons of Rachel, had a close relationship with his father: "And when his brethren saw that their father loved him more than all his brethren, they hated him, and could not speak peaceably unto him."[4] A sequence of additional events (gossiping and telling his brothers about dreams that portrayed him as a family leader) contributed to additional hatred by his brothers: "And they hated him yet the more for his dreams, and for his words."[5] When an opportunity arose that he was alone with them far away from home, they plotted to kill him. Judah (fourth son of Leah) saved Joseph's life by suggesting that

---

3 For more details on this episode, consult Genesis 37:1–28.

4 Genesis 37:4. All biblical translations are from the Jewish Publication Society of America Version of the Tanakh (1917).

5 Genesis 37:8.

they sell him to a caravan going to Egypt. There, he was again traded as a slave. In this second episode, brotherly hatred changed Joseph's status from that of a seventeen-year-old prince in his homeland to that of a helpless slave exiled in a foreign land.

Third Hatred-Exile Episode: The Egyptian Exile

The hatred-exile relationship did not end with Joseph. It affected several generations of the Jewish people through an inescapable cascade of events.

Joseph became viceroy of Egypt, the brothers were reconciled and reunited, Jacob and his children and grandchildren moved to Egypt because Joseph was viceroy and could not leave Egypt, and also because there was a severe famine in the land of Canaan.[6] Jacob's children and grandchildren, who numbered seventy individuals, initially settled in a region called Goshen. Later, Jacob's descendants multiplied and spread throughout Egypt. A new king arose who initiated a systematic program of persecution and enslavement of the Hebrews (as they were known at the time). When Moses led them out of Egypt, they numbered 600,000 men, bringing the total count of the Jewish people at the time to approximately three million individuals. At that point, this people needed a land to call their own. That land had been promised to their forefathers, who were already buried there. This is how the Jewish people ended up being born in exile outside their land.

Jewish People in and out of the Land of Israel

After a forty-year stay in the Sinai desert, the promise was realized and the Jewish people entered the Land of Israel led by Joshua. Under the leadership of the judges, the kings, and the prophets, they became a true

---

6 For more details on this episode, consult Genesis 47:1, 11–13, 27.

nation on its own land. After living there for approximately 850 years,[7] they were defeated and exiled by the Babylonians. Fortunately, they had a prophecy that this exile would last only seventy years, and indeed, at the end of that period, they were allowed to return to Israel. Under the leadership of Ezra and Nehemia, the 42,360 Jews who returned reorganized themselves in Israel, built the Second Temple, and resided there for approximately 422 years. Then the phenomenon of widespread baseless hatred emerged. In the year 70 CE, the Jewish people formally lost their sovereignty over the Land of Israel for a second time.

The Romans were not just conquerors seeking subjugation of the local population. Somehow, they had designs on the future of Jewish identity, because they attempted to erase all traces of the relationship between the Jewish people and its land by "ploughing the Temple Mount" and by calling the land Palestine. Jews ended up with no land for nineteen centuries, until May 14, 1948, when it became possible for them to return to the Land of Israel. In summary, when we tally all these episodes, we find that because of baseless hatred, the Jews had lived much longer outside Israel then inside (nineteen versus thirteen centuries, respectively).

Jewish Attitude toward Hatred

Consistent with a history profoundly marked by a hatred-exile relationship, traditional Jewish literature is unanimous in considering hatred a detestable human trait. There is a long list of sources, too long to be listed here. Hatred has been called "the ugliest of human traits" and is seen as the source of most human problems. Modern scholars consider

---

7 There is a disagreement among Jewish historians about the exact date of the destruction of the First Temple by the Babylonians.

it "an emotion that can only hurt mankind."[8] This unanimity goes all the way back to Sinai and is based on one explicit commandment: "Thou shalt not hate thy brother in thy heart."[9] A unique characteristic of this prohibition is that it actually provides a step-by-step recipe to navigate a conflictual situation and avoid the emergence of hatred. It also addresses the consequences of transgression, such as taking revenge or holding a grudge. In addition it provides unique insights into the love-hate relationship. To begin to address the underpinnings of baseless hatred, we need to review this prohibition and its methodology.

Principal Focus

The principal focus of the prohibition against hating a fellow Jew is about harboring hidden feelings of hatred (in the heart), feelings that are not expressed to the object of hate. To understand the full scope of this prohibition let us reexamine scenario 1.1, "The Full Plate."

Shimon sees Reuven at a buffet and makes a comment on his plate. Reuven feels insulted and hurt. The prohibition against hatred focuses on Reuven's reaction, even before he stared back at Shimon and returned to his wife. Internally, Reuven considered the comment an affront and transformed himself into a "victim," which justified ill feelings toward Shimon. All this occurred at the speed of light, almost unconsciously. That rapid process is the focus of this prohibition: although Reuven's reaction occurred in a split second, he is not allowed to justify it by the fact that it is an emotional "reflex." He is expected to be aware of that process and stop it. Emotion is no justification for destroying a relationship with another Jew without any examination.

---

8 Nachum Amsel, *The Jewish Encyclopedia of Moral and Ethical Issues* (Northvale, NJ: Jason Aronson, 1994), 91.

9 This commandment and the following injunctions are found in Leviticus 19:17–18.

Another unique aspect of this prohibition is that it directs itself at only one of the two parties in the incident: the one who feels victimized. Whether Shimon's action was warranted is not relevant here (it will be addressed in the last two chapters of this book, and Jewish law addresses these issues as well). Please note also that the basis for Reuven's feelings is not a key criterion: we know that they were based on perception and misplaced causality (see chapter 1's discussion of scenario 1.1). But he would also be expected to stop his feelings of hatred if Shimon had definitely insulted him instead of merely making a trivial comment. The expectation of Jewish law is zero tolerance for retaliatory ill feelings that can turn into hatred. As we learned in the previous chapter, if feelings of hatred are allowed to take root, they will have staying power and become practically irreversible. To help Reuven achieve the desired objective, there is a second phase that includes five complementary injunctions.

Five Injunctions

1. "You shall reprove your fellow." This reproof means that in scenario 1.1, Reuven should go back to Shimon as soon as possible and attempt a dialogue regarding the incident. But, since Reuven has been hurt, this communication with Shimon puts him on a dangerous course. Reuven is not given a license to speak to Shimon with an accusatory tone or to reprimand him. The way this dialogue is approached is critical and is addressed by the next injunction.

2. "And do not bear a sin because of him." This means that Reuven must approach Shimon with extreme sensitivity and certainly not embarrass him. For example, Reuven is not allowed to say, "Who gave you the right to comment on what I eat? Who do you think you are?" Reuven's attitude should be sincere and respectful, with the intention of seeking a solution.

This communication has an important objective for both individuals.

It helps Reuven, because as soon as he speaks about the issue – thereby causing his emotions to become more circumscribed and rational – he rescues it from the realm of his inner emotions, where it would fester and become uncontrollable. When he makes the effort to communicate his feelings to Shimon, Reuven is forced to formulate his thoughts in a rational and precise way. Describing his experience of the incident to Shimon, who was obviously also present and brings his own perspective, allows the incident to acquire finite dimensions in Reuven's eyes. For example, if Shimon answered, "What I said was only meant as a joke and I never had any intention of hurting you," Reuven should realize that the issue is trivial and should not be given any importance.

While Reuven speaks to Shimon with the intention of calming his own emotions, the dialogue also benefits Shimon because Reuven explains to Shimon that he cares about him. Reuven expresses that he felt hurt only because Shimon is important to him. When Shimon hears those words uttered sincerely, he will probably feel better about his relationship with Reuven. At the end, if the communication is done with care, the "reproof" strengthens the relationship between the two parties.

If Shimon accepts this sensitive rebuke, Reuven is required to forgive Shimon completely and immediately. This implies that he should not mention it to Shimon at a later time. Also, he should not remember it or to talk about it to anyone else. With such an outcome, the case should be closed. The objective of stopping the emergence of hatred has been accomplished.

If, however, Shimon refuses the sensitive rebuke, Reuven must make several attempts and find a better approach to reach an understanding.

What if Reuven refuses to approach Shimon? He will fall into one or two traps: he will want to take revenge or he will keep a grudge. These outcomes are addressed in the third and fourth injunctions.

3. "You shall not take revenge." The normal reaction of a person who is hurt or harmed by another is to correct the injustice and to seek to "pay back" the perpetrator: it seems "only fair." This type of reaction should be avoided. It is important to note that naturally, "we all have a strong sense of fairness,"[10] and our capacity to be altruistic or empathetic toward others wanes rapidly when they have behaved unfairly.

Scenario 2.1: David's Daughter's Wedding

David's daughter is getting married. While working on the guest list with his wife, he tells her, "We are not inviting the Cohen family! Remember, they did not invite us to their son's wedding eight years ago!" It does not matter to David that the Cohens did not intend to cause any ill feelings (they were facing budget limitations and their daughter in-law's family was very large). Although David did not know those facts, all that counts for him is that he expected to be invited and was not. He felt betrayed and his pride was hurt because other friends were invited. After eight years, David cannot miss the opportunity to retaliate.

4. "You shall not bear a grudge against the children of your people." In the case of David's daughter's wedding, the situation may play out in one of several ways. Scenario 2.2 is one possible outcome.

Scenario 2.2: David Carries a Grudge

David does not retaliate and actually decides to invite the Cohen family. The invitations are sent out and it happens that David

---

10 Frith, *Making Up the Mind*, 190–91.

meets Mr. Cohen after the latter has received the invitation.
Mr. Cohen says to David, "Mazal tov! We are delighted that
your daughter is getting married this spring!" David responds:
"Thank you! You see, we invited you, we are not like you."

Here, David kept a grudge. He was expected to make a positive effort to forgive and to completely erase the incident from his memory. Instead, he simply remained passive. In the absence of any action on David's part to dislodge his immediate negative reaction to the original incident, his primitive neural system stored this event in his long-term memory as a hurtful and threatening event, and David nurtured a grudge.

Another version of keeping a grudge is "going silent."

Scenario 2.3: Going Silent

Suppose that after scenario 1.1, Reuven decides not to approach
Shimon to seek an understanding: he feels so insulted that he
decides not to speak to Shimon at all and just to ignore him. He
may invoke excuses such as wishing to avoid a confrontation and
keeping his distance to have "peace." All these are unacceptable
excuses. This course of action is considered reprehensible
for multiple reasons. First, by refusing to give Shimon any
consideration, Reuven displays arrogance and disdain for his
friend. Most importantly, this behavior is reprehensible because
Reuven's silent treatment triggers what is called "the mirror
effect." Shimon will eventually see Reuven's cold silent treatment
and will react likewise. This process results in amplifying the
hatred by creating reciprocal hatred, emanating from Shimon
toward Reuven.

5. "You shall love your fellow as yourself." Does this mean that in the original scenario 1.1, Reuven was expected to switch from feeling

insulted by Shimon's comment to feeling love toward him? No, Reuven was not. The imposition of a "love requirement" in this context is all about avoiding hatred. To fully understand it, we must have recourse to the explanation provided by the brilliant sage Hillel, who reformulated the love commandment as follows: "That which is hateful to you, do not do to others."[11] This translation of love to avoiding hatred opens several insights into the misunderstood love-hate relationship and addresses Reuven in these terms:

A. The reason you were expected to dialogue with Shimon and not to retaliate or hold a grudge is because of a fundamental bond between you and him. But this bond is not about loving him like yourself at the moment he insults you; it is about a "minimum" loving behavior. If you feel hurt by Shimon and feel that your love for him has vanished, the least you can do is to not hate him, since you yourself would hate to be hated. If you make the effort not to hate him when you feel victimized, you are expressing love!

B. When the above "love" expression is viewed in the context of stopping hatred, the terminology "as yourself" means that since you cannot (should not) hate yourself, you should not hate him. The emergence of hatred requires a "devaluation" or "dehumanization" of the object of hate, and you cannot do that to yourself. Also, by refraining from hatred, you end up saving yourself from inner destruction and, ironically, expressing love toward yourself. In summary, "You shall love your fellow as yourself" has been called a "golden rule" not because it represents an appeal to indiscriminate love but because it constitutes a powerful tool to prevent the spread of hatred.

Parenthetically, it is interesting to note the parallel between the

---

11   Babylonian Talmud, *Shabbat* 31a.

love-hate formulation of Hillel (first century BCE) and what is stated by Robert and Karin Sternberg in their book on the nature of hate: "Hate and love have, in many cases, been studied in isolation from each other. It may seem odd, in a book on hate, to review a theory of love! But central to our theory is the notion that love and hate are closely related, and that, to understand the one, it helps to understand the other."[12] (Also see chapter 1.)

Summary

This analysis showed that based on historical facts, there is a deep relationship between hatred among Jews and exile from the Land of Israel. That link began during the "fetal" phase of the Jewish people when it was made of a few families; it was present when these families developed into a people in Egypt and continued throughout its history. The hatred-exile connection became a sort of existential paradigm that holds the key to unanswered questions about the mysterious nature of the Jewish people, its survival, and its recent return to the Land of Israel after nineteen centuries.

Consistent with the hatred-exile paradigm, hatred among Jews is considered a serious and severe human trap for which there is zero tolerance. We are now ready to ask: Why focus on baseless hatred? And what makes hatred baseless?

---

12 Sternberg and Sternberg, *The Nature of Hate*, 53.

3

Baseless Hatred: Causes and Consequences

Chapter 1 provided a general background on hatred drawn from psychology and neurobiology. Chapter 2 showed that the Jewish people have had a historical relationship with hatred. We also learned that Jews are expected to adhere to strict criteria regarding the emergence and manifestations of hatred in their interpersonal relationships. If that is so, why is it that the Talmudic sages focused on the notion of baseless hatred as a profound moral failure with long-lasting consequences? Somehow we still need to differentiate between generic and baseless hatred. To do that we will start by examining what causes hatred.

Let us consider scenario 1.1, where Shimon sees Reuven's full plate and says to him, "Reuven, you must be hungry!" In this encounter, Shimon was the "aggressor" and Reuven was the "victim." When Reuven decides to end his relationship with Shimon and nurse feelings of resentment, the roles are reversed: the individual who felt victimized during the encounter (Reuven) now becomes the aggressor because he is the perpetrator of hate, while the individual who was the original aggressor (Shimon) becomes the victim of hate. This change occurs instantly because the victim feels justified by his perception that he was harmed unjustly. As we saw in chapter 1, this rapid response is the result of the work of the primitive neural system. Based on what we learned in chapter 2, and assuming that Shimon's statement that he had no intention of hurting Reuven was sincere, the answer to the question "who caused the hatred" is Reuven the hater, not Shimon.

Let us establish that all types of hatred have common features: hatred does not emerge in a vacuum, spontaneously, or randomly. Also, it does not come as a surprise to the hater. Hate is an emotional response, a reaction to some trigger. Triggers are misleading because they are chronologically the proximal cause to the emergence of hatred. But that does not make them acceptable. The differentiation between hatred and baseless hatred starts with an analysis of the causes of hatred and a judgment about their acceptability.

How Does It Happen and What Does It Look Like?

Triggers

Triggers can be divided into two types depending on whether or not they involve an encounter between the perpetrator and the victim of hate.

1. Triggers involving an encounter.

    A. *Verbal social interactions.* Hate can result from casual misspoken words that are misinterpreted. Two examples were given in chapter 1: scenario 1.1, "The Full Plate," and scenario 1.2, "The Wedding Dress." Those types of incidents are common occurrences among friends and family members in different types of social settings. Just about any comment or joke can become the source of anger on the part of the recipient, and that anger need not be expressed; it can be nursed in silence for a long time.

B. *Verbal social interactions with amplification.* Sometimes the reaction of a third party (a friend or a close family member) can contribute to amplifying the impact of the proximal cause.

Scenario 3.1: The Full Plate Amplified

Let us reconsider scenario 1.1, when Reuven walks back to his wife Sarah and expresses his anger at what Shimon said to him. Now, Sarah responds as follows: "How dare he speak to you in that way, after all you did for him before he was married! What an ingrate!" Sarah's reaction provokes additional rage in Reuven, which facilitates the emergence of hatred and encourages holding a grudge.

We saw in chapter 1 that very small triggers such as criticisms, jokes, or even facial expressions may eventually lead to a hatred response because they can be misinterpreted and perceived as aggression. The recipient feels hurt and trapped, and unleashes a primitive neural system response based on his or her insecurities. Such social interactions are considered invalid causes for hatred; any hatred that ensues is baseless.

C. *Business interactions.* Sometimes, the encounter between the two parties is the result of a normal commercial transaction.

Scenario 3.2: The Defective House

Moshe sells his house to Yitzhak. After living in the house, Yitzhak discovers some defects and develops the feeling that Moshe took advantage of him. Yitzhak behaves as a victim because of the perceived financial loss and thus "justifies" hatred toward Moshe. In his mind, the "cause" is Moshe's dishonesty.

Yitzhak did not bother to speak to Moshe about the issue and understand his point of view. Yitzhak was the sole judge of the situation and became persuaded that Moshe owed him money. Had he approached Moshe with an objective assessment of what he expected, and asked for the difference to be split, the issue could have been solved. The "cause" that Yitzhak uses to justify his hatred is not valid and it is another example of baseless hatred. Many business partnerships end with resentment and hatred that consumes not only the two parties but also their families.

2. Triggers that do not involve an encounter.

    A. *Hearsay and association.* Hatred can be triggered indirectly, without any hostile encounter even taking place.

Scenario 3.3: The Telltale Coworker

Shlomi, Avi, and Yaakov are friends. Avi and Yaakov work in the same office. Shlomi and Yaakov are at a wedding reception, and Yaakov, who has had a little too much to drink, tells Shlomi that, at the office, Avi spoke pejoratively about him and his flashy new car. Shlomi accepts this gossip as truth and reacts to it as a personal insult, saying to himself: "How could Avi dare to do such a thing? I thought he was my friend!" He feels betrayed and explodes in seething rage against Avi. This is a case of hatred by hearsay.

Scenario 3.4: The Offended Wife

This is a variation of scenario 1.1, "The Full Plate." This time

Shimon and Reuven are at a reception early in the morning, but
Reuven's wife Sarah could not attend. Shimon sees Reuven's full
plate and says to him, "Reuven, you must be hungry!" Reuven
returns home and relates the incident to Sarah. Unexpectedly,
Sarah becomes emotionally involved, feels personally insulted
by Shimon's comment and can no longer speak to him. In this
case, Sarah was not part of the incident and developed hatred
toward Shimon without any interaction with him. Her hatred was
all by hearsay and "allegiance" to her husband. This is a case
of hatred by hearsay and association.

Scenarios 3.3 and 3.4 are two cases of hatred by hearsay. They
illustrate the very strong relationship between gossip and
hatred. In scenario 3.3, the object of gossip (Shlomi) was also
the recipient of gossip (from Yaakov) and ended up hating the
original gossiper (Avi), who had spoken pejoratively about him
at the office. In scenario 3.4, it is the direct recipient of gossip
(Sarah) who became the hater. Gossip is a very potent generator
of hatred. It is particularly dangerous between individuals who
are peers or have some preexisting envy between them (see
below). These causes of hatred are invalid and both represent
cases of baseless hatred.

Parenthetically, the relationship between hatred and gossip is
so strong that it works also the other way around. A person
who hates finds it particularly easy to gossip about the object
of hate because the hater devalues that person and believes that
the person is bad or morally deficient. The point of intersection
between gossip and hatred is that both devalue people. This
relationship is further developed in chapters 9 and 10.

B. Propaganda. A clear example of baseless hatred is that which is evoked or provoked in individuals or in groups simply based on propaganda. "We understand that people's behavior is controlled by beliefs even if these beliefs are false. And we soon learn that we can control people's behavior by giving them false beliefs. This is the dark side of communication."[1] Propaganda can shape the perceptions of individuals or masses through the use of language (slogans), images (posters, symbols), fear, generalizations, simplifications, and name calling. Propaganda works even if it is based on untruths. It works more effectively when it comes from "friends" or individuals who are trusted, such as leaders, teachers, or parents. It is even more effective when it is accompanied by persuasion.

Using the impact of hatred, propagandists are able to achieve multiple goals, including the attainment of personal power or political objectives. Amazingly, propaganda can be effective whether or not the propagandists themselves believe it: they could be completely manipulative and still succeed. For our purposes, the efficacy of propaganda illustrates the general sensitivity that average people have for "mental viruses" that result in hatred. It also explains the success of the new worldwide BDS (boycott, divestment, sanctions) movement aimed at delegitimizing the State of Israel.[2]

What Makes Triggers Invalid Causes of Hatred

Triggers are not valid causes of hatred for several reasons. We learned in chapter 1 that hatred can be triggered by stimuli that are real or imagined. Also, the hater makes assessments that border on the irrational because he or she is driven by perceptions and generalized judgments

---

1   Frith, *Making Up the Mind*, 178.

2   See http://www.standwithus.com/BDS/.

and confuses association with causality. The above triggers work so well because they find a receptive audience: basic human emotions such as envy and jealousy, as well as other insecurities, predispose a person to react in an inflammatory manner. These feelings function as sitting receptors, ready to fire with extremely low thresholds. In the Jewish tradition,[3] these sentiments are considered human deficiencies and therefore invalid causes of hatred. Two examples, envy and jealousy, are particularly important because no one escapes them. Triggers of envy and jealousy are multiple:

1. A person may envy another because of his or her wealth.

2. There is a natural envy or competition among members of the same trade or profession. So when an average person sees that a colleague performs better, this average person may develop envy, but that reaction is based on insecurity.

3. The fact that a family member or a friend or a neighbor receives an honor or some type of public recognition can trigger envy. Many people do not react positively to the fact that a friend achieves fame or achieves a prestigious position. Instead of sharing in the happiness, they resent it. Here also, the trigger is insecurity about one's own status.

4. Another irrational basis for hatred arises when a person sees that a friend has positive personality traits that he does not possess.

5. One may resent the fact that his friend does not do him favors as he expects. For example, a person may expect to be invited to his friend's home or social events, or to receive more substantial gifts. Such resentment is the product of unfounded and unrealistic

---

3 Moshe Chaim Luzzatto, *Orchot Tzaddikim: The Ways of the Tzaddikim* (Nanuet, NY: Feldheim Publishers, 1995); Israel Meir haCohen Kagan, *Sefer Chafetz Chayim*, translated by Yedidya Levy (New York: Mazal Press, 2004).

expectations. These roots of human jealousy turn into low-threshold triggers of hatred.

Scenario 3.5: The Jealous Friend

Let us reconsider again scenario 1.1 with the following additional background to the relationship between Shimon and Reuven prior to their meeting at the buffet. They were "friends," but Reuven had accumulated substantial wealth in his Hong Kong–based electronics business, and Shimon envied Reuven's rapid success. Somehow, Shimon had expected that Reuven would share some of his wealth because of their friendship, but that did not occur. Shimon became slowly and silently resentful; what troubled him most was that when Reuven and his wife were invited to Shimon's house they brought "cheap" gifts. In the course of time, Shimon came to resent Reuven himself, not just his wealth, but Reuven was totally unaware of what was being fabricated in Shimon's mind.

That background preceded their meeting at the buffet: Shimon finds Reuven in a vulnerable position because the latter is obese and his plate is full. Shimon takes advantage of the situation and teases him, saying, "Reuven, you must be hungry!" This is why Reuven is surprised. His pride is hurt and he stares back at Shimon in disbelief. Shimon's comment unleashes an immediate defensive reaction from Reuven, who decides to avoid Shimon and not talk to him. This is a case of baseless hatred because in the whole cascade of events that lead to it, there was not one element to justify it.

The same applies to all the triggers and apparent causes listed above (misspoken words, social interactions, business interactions). They can be based on silent envy and common jealousy of which we are not aware. In the Jewish tradition, these causes are unacceptable because they constitute seeds of hatred. Unsatisfied needs and desires can never be fulfilled by others; they must be controlled by the person who experiences them. Individuals who do not work at controlling envy or jealousy can turn into time bombs ready to explode at the smallest trigger. If they develop any hatred, there is no other cause for it except themselves.

Is Hate Ever Warranted or Acceptable?

Whether one considers the opinion of the sages or that of social scientists with expertise in the field of hatred, there is a broad consensus that the objective is not to condemn hatred in all circumstances and attempt to eradicate it completely (assuming it were possible). Hatred is a built-in defense mechanism with a valid purpose: to help us avoid threats to our survival. The best illustration of the Jewish position on hatred comes from the famous section of the book Ecclesiastes (3:8) that begins with "To everything there is a season…" There, it states: "A time to love and a time to hate." It is permitted to hate one's enemies, especially during times of war (even though one may not rejoice when one's enemy falls).

Similarly, hatred experts indicate that the goal is obviously not to eliminate all influence of the primitive neural system, because it is the source of important emotions (love, fear, joy, anger). The objective is to become aware that it is capable of extreme responses and those must be zealously kept in check.

The Five Characteristics of Baseless Hatred

There are five aspects of hatred that make it baseless and gratuitous. Four are characteristics of generic hatred that are unacceptable from a Jewish standpoint and therefore make it baseless. The fifth one is linked directly to the national bond that unites Jews and is addressed below separately under the Judah principle of mutual responsibility.

1. *Hatred is a response that is unfair, unjust, and excessive.* In most cases, the apparent causes of hatred are revealed to be trivial after objective examination. In the mind of the hater they are infinitely magnified based on inaccurate perceptions and misplaced causality. They are fueled by the hater's insecurities, to which he or she is oblivious.

   In terms of consequences, hatred has been appropriately called "the nuclear weapon of the mind."[4] It is an excessive and unfair response: the object of hate is immediately devalued and characterized as an enemy; that person could be suffering and the hater would have no empathy. That is an excessive and unjust response because the hater does not seek justice but revenge, and even annihilation. As a response, hatred is equivalent to burning down the neighbors' house just because they allowed their dog to dirty your yard.

2. *Hatred is avoidable through the path of dialogue.* Independent of the nature of the trigger, the hater could have used a step-by-step, reliable path to resolution (as detailed in chapter 2). Most triggers are so subjective that simple discussion would expose them and allow a resolution. But the hater refused to make the effort to bring the issue to light. Instead the hater allowed the primitive neural system to control him or her and therefore felt justified in becoming antagonistic and vindictive. He or she ignored the path of peace. This hatred could have been avoided and is therefore baseless.

3. *Hatred lasts.* Once hatred develops, it does not disappear; the primitive neural system provides the individual with memory mechanisms that perpetuate the original offense independent of the

---

4   Dozier, *Why We Hate*, 1.

time elapsed. Any pain that was perceived at the time of the incident remains vivid for years, as if it had just occurred. Hatred is a "stable emotional pattern," even considered by some to be irreversible. The consequence is that hatred is felt today for events that took place years ago. Thus the hatred manifested today is baseless because it is completely disconnected from its origin.

4. *Hatred spreads.* Initially, hatred originates in the brain of the hater unbeknownst to the object of hate. The hater believes that his hate is well hidden, but eventually, he has no choice but to show it because of the urge to retaliate. Even if he avoids interactions with the object of hate, that object will automatically retaliate and becomes a perpetrator of hate. Family members of this new perpetrator may also be hurt and join in this reciprocal hate. The result is that the original hate spreads like a contagious disease from the mind of the hater, infecting multiple reciprocal haters. Independent of the "cause" of the original hate, all this additional reciprocal hate is also baseless.

5. *Hatred destroys the national bond of mutual responsibility (*arevut*).* The first four characteristics were generically applicable to everyone. This is the specifically Jewish characteristic of baseless hatred and requires a separate discussion.

Sinat Chinam: A Jewish Concern

Hatred among any two Jews is not considered a private matter. It is viewed as having serious consequences for the entire body of the Jewish people, because it destroys the national bond of inter-individual mutual responsibility called *arevut*. As outlined in the Talmud, it can be expressed as "Every Jew is responsible for every other Jew."[5] *Arevut* is considered the glue or the cement that binds Jews together to form one people; it is at the core of peoplehood and national identity. Throughout history, it has kept Jews connected even when they were exiled and dispersed. Baseless hatred and *arevut* are mutually exclusive: baseless hatred destroys *arevut* and *arevut* constitutes the remedy for baseless hatred. One is the antithesis of the other. To appreciate this reciprocal relationship, we need to understand the origins of *arevut*.

Origins of *Arevut*: The Judah Principle

Arevut represents a commitment to mutual responsibility that must exist among Jews. It is not an idealistic concept. In fact, it did not come naturally but as the result of a struggle. It arose during a moment of unprecedented crisis that threatened to destroy the first family that was destined to give birth to the Jewish people: that of Jacob.

The idea of mutual responsibility was the subject of a clash between Jacob's two adult sons Joseph and Judah during their first recorded dialogue.[6] The dialogue took place under strange circumstances, in Egypt, while Joseph was the man in charge of the food supply of that country (he was the wheat czar for Egypt and the region). There was a famine in Canaan and all of Joseph's brothers (except Benjamin) had come to Egypt to buy wheat. When they came in front of the wheat czar, they did not recognize the individual they had sold as a slave twenty-two years before; they only saw an Egyptian viceroy. However, Joseph recognized them, and set up a test for his brothers to see whether they had repented of their hateful behavior toward him. He accused them of being spies, and he imprisoned Shimon and indicated that he would remain

---

5   *Shevuot* 39a. The Hebrew word *arevut* will be used interchangeably with the term "mutual responsibility" throughout this book.

6   See Genesis 44:16–34.

in jail until the other brothers would return to Egypt with Benjamin in order to authenticate their claims. Then he sent them on their way with food for their families (and also frightened them by returning the money they had paid for the food).

When they returned with Benjamin, Shimon was freed and Joseph provided them with additional ample food stores and sent all the brothers on their way home. But he fabricated a situation through which Benjamin was found guilty of stealing the viceroy's personal goblet. The brothers knew that Benjamin was not a thief and that the situation was contrived. They knew they were being set up, but were helpless in front of the evidence. Judah emerged and engaged Joseph in a one-on-one argument, basing his position on the concept of *arevut*.

There was no disagreement about the facts of the case. Both sides agreed that Joseph's goblet was found in Benjamin's sac and that the latter was caught red-handed. To test the brothers' sense of responsibility to their youngest brother, Benjamin, Joseph announced that his verdict was that Benjamin should remain as a slave. Judah accepted that the verdict was fair. He first requested that they all remain as slaves instead of Benjamin. That was rejected by Joseph as unjust. Joseph said: "The man in whose hand the goblet was found, he shall be my slave" (Genesis 44:17). Judah then pleaded with Joseph on behalf of his father, who would be distraught at the loss of Benjamin, and explained that he had taken responsibility for Benjamin's return; therefore he offered himself instead of his brother: "Please let me stay as your slave instead of the young man" (Genesis 44:33).

The brothers passed Joseph's test. Joseph presented them with a verdict based on the concept of individual responsibility: only Benjamin would be jailed. The verdict seemed fair and just. But unlike the situation many years before when they had judged their brother Joseph and abandoned him to an unknown fate, now the brothers stood up for Benjamin and offered to go to jail instead of him. Judah upheld the concept of *arevut*: "I am my brother's keeper." I gave myself as a guarantor for my brother so that we could all survive, Judah avows, so I will die for him if necessary. At this point Joseph tearfully revealed himself to his brothers and the family was reunited.

Jews in the Disapora, Jews in the Land of Israel

When Joseph was in Israel, he was a dreamer; when he was in exile, he became a master at turning dreams into reality – his own and those of others (Pharaoh and his two chamberlains).[7] Joseph was a smashing success. Furthermore, his success was not limited to the material realm. His moral stature was impeccable. When Potiphar's wife tried to seduce him, he succeeded where most men would have failed (which gave him the permanent title of *Tzaddik*, Righteous). Finally, in spite of his high position, he kept his Jewish identity and did not assimilate into Egyptian high society. This is how Joseph became a prototype of the "successful" Diaspora Jew.

Judah was the prototype of Jew who succeeds at home, in Israel. Judah lived in the land of Canaan, next to his family. He confronted several difficult family challenges and overcame all of them in a masterful way. But he never took the easy path. Early on, Judah challenged his older brothers and saved Joseph's life by suggesting that they sell him rather than kill him.

In the episode described above, when all the brothers came back from Egypt with food and Shimon had been jailed, the family was in total disarray: two brothers had disappeared (Joseph and Shimon) and the father, Jacob, refused unequivocally to send Benjamin. The whole family

---

7 Genesis, chapters 40–41.

was at a standstill, not knowing what to do. All attempts to convince the father, including that of the oldest brother Reuben, had failed. Again, Judah emerged with authority and saved the day. Judah knew not to speak to his father until all the food had been exhausted. Even then, he waited for Jacob to bring up the issue. At that point, Judah stood up and articulated wisely and respectfully to his father the only two available choices: either send Benjamin or starve.

But Judah did more than present an analysis: he created a novel solution by implicating himself in an unprecedented way. He put his honor and his life at risk by telling his father essentially: *I am his guarantor, I assume full responsibility for him.* On Judah's word, Jacob surrendered instantly and took the chance of letting Benjamin travel to Egypt. At that point, Judah had invented the notion of *arevut*. By his action, Judah opened a path that would transform Jewish history. When Benjamin was caught red-handed with Joseph's goblet, Judah challenged the Egyptian viceroy with the same argument: I am my brother's keeper. When Joseph saw that Judah was ready to die for his brother, history took a pause; all role-playing ended and Joseph revealed himself. Judah and his *arevut* solution had won.

Joseph's Legacy

As described in chapter 2, the Jews were destined to be in exile for most of their history, and Joseph left them a legacy with multiple messages.

1. In the Diaspora, a Jew can build a lot, but what is built does not last. After Joseph died, the status he had achieved for himself and his people in Egypt evaporated because a new king arose who did not know Joseph. The Egyptians no longer recognized or acknowledged Joseph's contributions to Egyptian society, and felt no compunction about enslaving his people. History has shown that any accomplishments or contributions of Diaspora Jews did not protect

them from genocides (parenthetically, when Herzl reached this same conclusion – years before decorated German Jewish veterans of World War I were led to the gas chambers by the country they had served – he became driven with the idea that the Jews had no hope in the Diaspora and needed a homeland).

2. In the Diaspora, Joseph kept his love for the Land of Israel intact. On his deathbed, he commanded the Hebrews to bring back his bones to Israel when they would be freed.

3. Joseph's love of the Land of Israel was transmitted to his descendants. Even after five generations, the five daughters of Tselofchad loved the Land of Israel so much that they challenged the order of the day by asking that, as women, they should have the right to inherit a portion of the Land of Israel.[8] They succeeded not just for women's rights but because of their love for the Land of Israel.

4. Finally, for those interested in the teachings of numerology, the name Joseph has the same numerical value (156) as Zion in Hebrew.

Judah's Legacy: The Judah Principle

1. Judah left the following legacy: when hatred becomes malignant and threatens to destroy families (at that time, the kernel of the whole Jewish people), the solution is mutual responsibility, *arevut*. That was the Judah principle. When Judah created *arevut* it became a solution not just for the hatred that had torn his family at the time, but it remained as a legacy for their descendants who were going to be enslaved in Egypt.

2. Judah taught that in order to return and live in Israel, the Jewish people must reestablish its commitment to mutual responsibility. They did so at the covenant at Sinai.

---

8 For full details, consult Numbers, chapter 27.

3. Before dying, Jacob blessed his children, the twelve tribes. To Judah, he gave the blessing of kingship precisely because Judah originated the Judah principle and reunited the family. In Jewish tradition, the role of the king is to rally and unite the whole nation in a common direction.

4. In the Hebrew language, the word "Jew" is *Yehudi,* meaning a descendent of Judah or a participant in the Judah principle.

This is how *arevut* was born and became the cement that held the Jewish people together later in its history.

Baseless Hatred Is a Jewish Concern because It Destroys *Arevut*

The fundamental *arevut* requirement among Jews gives to baseless hatred a national dimension. The reason is simple: a person who hates is unable to feel empathy for the person who is the target of hate, as we learned: "The capacity for empathy is centered in…one of the most advanced areas of the brain.… Personalized thinking tends to suppress empathy for others and focus on oneself and one's perceived emotional needs."[9] Without empathy, *arevut* is impossible to achieve. Therefore, achieving the goal of mutual responsibility requires a high level of training of the capacities of the advanced neural system, to see the humanity of others and accept the uniqueness of each individual (see chapter 10). That is a requirement of Jewish identity.

Hatred between two Jews results in a tear that does not stop at their relationship. It reverberates and ultimately destroys the unity and integrity of the national fabric. When that process spreads, it turns one people into a group of individuals and the cohesiveness of the Jewish people dissolves away. One image is that all Jews are considered to be in one boat. Any person who hates another makes a hole on his side of

---

9 Dozier, *Why We Hate,* 231.

the boat; the whole boat sinks. As baseless hatred is a poison and threat to Jewish unity, it is a major Jewish concern.

The Historical Role of Baseless Hatred in Jewish Life

Based on the above five characteristics, I propose the following definition of baseless hatred: Baseless hatred is an unfair, excessive, and avoidable reaction by one Jew that transforms another Jew into an enemy and thereby destroys the integrity of the Jewish people.

Now that we have a crystallized definition of baseless hatred, we can test it by reviewing the three hatred-exile episodes described in chapter 2, as well as a fourth hatred-exile episode: the current exile.

First hatred-exile episode: hatred of Esau toward Jacob. Although Esau had a reason to feel disappointed, he could have attempted a dialogue with his brother. A dialogue immediately after the incident of the blessing might have resulted in a resolution even with a separation. But Esau just followed the path of hate and planned in his heart to kill his brother, leaving no room for resolution.

The hatred of Esau fits the criteria described above: it was unfair and excessive (death is not the appropriate punishment for a lost blessing), and it was long-lasting.[10]

Second hatred-exile episode: hatred of Joseph's brothers toward him. Similarly, the hatred of Joseph's brothers appeared to have multiple

---

10   When Jacob and Esau are reunited in Genesis 33:4 and share a brotherly embrace, the word "kissed" is written in the Torah text with dots on all the letters to indicate something unusual about the word. Opinions differ on what this means. Some Talmudic sages say that the dots, which usually signify that something is missing from the text, indicate that the kiss was not sincere. The Tannaitic sage Rabbi Shimon bar Yochai explains in this regard that it is axiomatic that Esau hates Jacob, but here something unusual happened and his heart was softened such that he gave a genuine kiss.

causes based on Joseph's behavior (preferential treatment by the father, Joseph's dreams of domination). Yet it fits the definition of baseless hatred, because the brothers refused to speak to Joseph. If they had attempted a dialogue, they could have helped him improve his behavior and together reached a mature understanding. Here also, it was unfair and excessive (they wanted to kill him), and it was avoidable – the path of dialogue and understanding would have succeeded because we know that Joseph cared greatly about his brothers; we also know that the concern of the brothers lasted until after the death of Jacob.[11]

Third hatred-exile episode: the Egyptian exile. Beyond the circumstances that led to the emigration of Jacob's family to Egypt, his descendants remained there and were unfairly subjected to harsh treatment and slavery by Pharaoh. When Moses became an adult, he identified greatly with the plight of his enslaved brothers and took large personal risks to alleviate their pain.[12] He wondered why the Jews had to be subjected to slavery. The answer came to him when he tried to resolve a dispute between two Jews: his efforts backfired and he realized that the Jews quarreled and slandered each other. The Jew that he rebuked was ready to denounce him to the authorities. Indeed Pharaoh sought to kill Moses and as a consequence, he had to go into exile for quite some time in the land of Midian.[13] This was another instance where internecine dispute led to exile.

Fourth hatred-exile episode: the destruction of the Second Temple. The longest exile, of course, is the current one, which resulted in there being no independent Jewish government in the Land of Israel from 70 CE

---

11 The brothers worried when Jacob died that Joseph would no longer have a reason to restrain himself from seeking revenge on them for what they had done to him. See Genesis 50:15.

12 For details consult Exodus 2:11.

13 For details consult Exodus 2:15.

until 1948. When the sages wanted to explain how baseless hatred led to the destruction of the Temple and of Jerusalem, and the long exile that ensued, they described a private party given by an unnamed man (the host). The host sent his messenger to invite his friend Kamtza but, by error, the messenger invited the host's enemy, a man named Bar Kamtza.[14] Bar Kamtza came to the party and was discovered by the host, who wanted to eject him. Bar Kamtza begged the host not to eject him in public, but the host hated him with such intensity that he threw him out. Bar Kamtza hoped that the sages who witnessed his humiliation would save him. Since they remained quiet, Bar Kamtza went and denounced all the Jews to the Roman emperor. This slander eventually led to the destruction and exile.

Conclusion

We have clarified some of the mystery associated with the terminology "baseless hatred." The fact that baseless hatred is an issue of special concern in a Jewish context does not in any way suggest that Jews have a unique propensity to hate without basis. The triggers of hatred are the same for Jews and non-Jews. Baseless hatred is a Jewish concern because its triggers – though universal in human experience – are not neutral events for Jews. Jewish tradition considers invalid and baseless all triggers that are rooted in a person's insecurities and feelings of envy.

In summary, baseless hatred is a Jewish concern for two independent sets of reasons: (1) the four main characteristics of hatred (excessive, avoidable, permanent, and spreading) make it baseless; (2) hatred is incompatible with the requirement of mutual responsibility and dissolves away the integrity of the Jewish people. These characteristics of hatred make it an issue of national concern.

---

14   For the detailed story, consult the translation by Rabbi Aryeh Kaplan entitled *The Story of Tisha B'Av* (New York: Moznaim, 1981), 19.

4

The Judah Principle: *Arevut*

Based on the definition of baseless hatred provided in the previous chapter, we now understand that "normal" hatred becomes "baseless" for several reasons: it is unfair, it is an excessive response, it is avoidable, it is not easily reversible, and it spreads. In addition, baseless hatred is a Jewish concern because of its lethal impact on the integrity of the Jewish people: it destroys the national bond of *arevut*.

In the last chapter we described the origin of *arevut* as it emerged in the life of Judah at the beginning of the formation of the Jewish people. In this chapter, we examine how *arevut* was incorporated during the formative years of the Jewish people and how it was permanently embedded in Jewish law and Jewish life. We also establish a connection between the loss of *arevut* and the catastrophes that befell the Jewish people around the year 70 CE. That connection is consistent with the link established by the sages of the Talmud between baseless hatred and the longest exile in Jewish history (as described in the introduction).

From this point forward we will discuss hate (or hatred) in the context of baseless hatred between Jews.

Arevut in the Formative Years of the Jewish People

Covenant

At the most critical moment in their history, Jews made a formal commitment to mutual responsibility. As described in chapter 2, the Jews left Egypt in 1312 BCE, and emerged as a large people of approximately three million individuals. Fifty days later, they arrived at the foot of Mount Sinai ready to receive the Torah and officially become one people. Before that revelation could take place, the Jews made a commitment of mutual responsibility that was officially recorded. The expression used to describe this unique feeling of unity was that they encamped at the foot of the mountain "as one man with one heart"[1] and they spoke with one voice. At the moment of the formal covenant with God they had to be united: a covenant with individuals would have no meaning. This was articulated by Rabbi Jonathan Sacks: "The covenant is more than a series of vertical commitments linking individual Jews with God. It is also a set of horizontal bonds linking Jews with one another in a collective responsibility."[2] At the most significant moment in the history of the Jewish people, the commitment to *arevut* was officially ratified.

The Next Forty Years

Following the Sinai covenant, the Jewish people traveled in the desert for forty years that were formative in many ways. They had two leaders who were model teachers of *arevut*.

---

1   Rashi, commentary on Exodus 19:2.

2   Jonathan Sacks, *One People? Tradition, Modernity, and Jewish Unity* (Portland, OR: The Littman Library of Jewish Civilization, 1993), 207.

Moses: Egyptian prince and prophet. As soon as he became an adult, Moses ignored his status of Egyptian prince and was drawn to his enslaved people.[3] He went to them wanting to share and alleviate their burdens. He stood against injustice when one of his brothers was being harassed by an Egyptian and when two Jews were fighting. Even when he had to run away, he arrived in a foreign land (Midian) and defended the daughters of Jethro against injustice.

Moses became the most eminent prophet who was privileged to have the closest encounter with God. A man with such a high level of spirituality was nevertheless constantly devoted to the smallest needs of his people. He would sit all day administering justice, dealing with all their issues, however mundane.[4] Even when the Jewish people behaved in rebellious ways, he took their side and pleaded their case. He showed time and again that his love for his people was boundless. At the end of his life, after forty years of leadership, he concluded by blessing them.[5] From the onset of his career until his last day, Moses behaved with the utmost empathy toward his people.

Where did he acquire this trait?

The empathy that Moses displayed came from the contributions of three exceptional women who excelled in empathy: his biological mother, Yocheved; his adoptive mother, Bithiah (Pharaoh's daughter, called in Hebrew Batya); and his sister, Miriam. Early on, when Yocheved and Miriam functioned as midwives,[6] they had demonstrated their empathy for babies by refusing to enforce Pharaoh's decree that all male babies

---

3 See Exodus 2:11–19.

4 See Exodus 18:13.

5 This episode is found in Deuteronomy 33:1–29.

6 According to Midrash the biblical midwives Shifra and Puah (Exodus 1:15) were none other than Yocheved and Miriam.

born to the Hebrews should be killed (Exodus 1:15–21).

Miriam was instrumental in convincing her father, Amram, to remarry her mother, Yocheved; they had divorced after Pharaoh had issued a decree against giving birth to Jewish males.[7] When they remarried and had a son, Yocheved saw the baby and decided to violate Pharaoh's decree and hide him.[8] In doing so, she took great risks because Pharaoh's decree was also enforced by the population. When Yocheved was forced to put the three-month-old Moses in a basket next to the reeds, Miriam could not let go. She stayed there to watch over him and thus was able to speak to Pharaoh's daughter after she pulled him from the reeds; Miriam offered to secure a nurse for the baby, and in this way ensured that baby Moses would be nursed by his own mother, Yocheved.

Bithiah, Pharaoh's daughter, also was a true heroine. When she saw this abandoned Jewish boy crying, she had compassion on him and kept him alive. She adopted him as her son, thus challenging the decree of her own father. Bithiah earned the merit of having given to Moses his name. Thus, Yocheved, Bithiah, and Miriam were three women all exceptional for their empathy. Moses was an exceptional leader because he had received a triple dose of empathy from these amazing women.

Aharon: high priest and peace maker. Aharon was Moses' older brother. Early on, Aharon showed that he had the remarkable trait of rejoicing for someone else's success: when his younger brother Moses was selected

---

7 Pharaoh knew through his magicians that a male redeemer would be born among the Hebrews, and he wanted to prevent his birth (see Rashi's commentary on Exodus 1:16). According to Midrash, Amram and Yocheved separated to prevent the birth of a baby boy, but Miriam successfully argued with her parents that while Pharaoh wanted to prevent baby boys from being born among the Hebrews, their separation served to prevent either a baby boy or a baby girl from being born, and thus actually worsened Pharaoh's decree.

8 This episode is found in Exodus 2:2–9.

to be the leader of the Jewish people, Aharon was happy for him.[9] In addition to his official duties as high priest, Aharon loved peace and pursued it not as an abstract ideal but as a real goal among his people. He worked diligently at helping average Jews resolve disputes and misunderstandings. He understood that those small disagreements could degenerate into unwarranted discord and hatred. He also understood that one must relate to people on their terms, not just on an esoteric spiritual plane. With his behavior, Aharon showed that bringing Jews closer to each other was simply an extension of his function as high priest since a main purpose of sacrifices was to bring Jews closer to God.

Entry into Israel

After the forty years in the desert, Joshua became the successor of Moses, and the Jewish people arrived for the first time in their land under the leadership of their new leader. At that critical time, the notion of mutual responsibility was manifested publicly. When they conquered Jericho and the city was consecrated, the whole people were held responsible for the sin of one person (Achan) who had appropriated some of the consecrated property for himself.

Also, when the land was shared among the tribes, two special arrangements are worthy of mention in the context of *arevut*: (1) The two tribes of Issachar and Zebulun made a pact whereby the people of Zebulun would become traders sailing far away while Issachar would devote their energies to the study of the Torah; Zebulun would support Issachar financially and would also receive one half of the spiritual benefit earned by Issachar's study. (2) Another arrangement was made such that the lands of the tribes of Judah and Benjamin were contiguous to share in hosting the Temple. (For the reason, see the discussion of the Ninth of Av below.)

---

9 This episode is found in Exodus 4:14.

Later in history, after the Jewish people lived in the Land of Israel, they entered the periods of the judges and the reigns of King David and King Solomon. Following the era of the judges, the notion of *arevut* suffered greatly. Eventually, the split of the Kingdom of Israel from the Kingdom of Judah led to the exile and disappearance of the Ten Tribes.

Arevut in Jewish Law

The notion of connectedness through mutual responsibility is a fundamental dimension of Jewish life, embedded in Jewish law and custom in numerous ways. As Rashi states the rabbinic principal in his commentary on Leviticus 26:37, "*Kol Yisrael arevim zeh lazeh*" (All of Israel are guarantors for [responsible for] one another). *Arevut* was embedded in numerous facets of Jewish law and only a few will be mentioned here.

Social Justice

A Jew is legally and morally bound to help any other Jew in need, whether the need is small or large, and certainly to help if another person is in danger.

The Hebrew word for charity is *tzedakah*, which means "justice." Providing for a needy person is viewed as performing a minimum act of justice. Jewish law is unequivocal about its importance. Everyone is obligated by this law (and there is a fixed percentage of one's income that one must give). Even a needy person has this obligation, such that two needy individuals are required to provide for each other even if it results in an exchange. The timing is critical: the person who delays providing to a needy person such that the status of the latter deteriorates is responsible for the consequences (whether physical or material). The method is also critical: one must be very careful to preserve the dignity of the recipient. For example, it is highly preferable that neither the donor nor the recipient know each other. In that context, the highest level of social justice is providing the needy person with a job or a loan because then the needy person is no longer just a recipient but a productive contributor.

To address these needs most Jewish communities set up a number of institutions for this purpose.

Returning a Lost Object

This is another example of legislation involving mutual responsibility. Any Jew passing by who comes upon a lost object (or a lost animal) does not have the freedom to walk by and consider that it is not his or her problem. A Jew is bound by law to see to it that any such object is kept safe and eventually returned to the rightful owner. The process involves also the responsibility for publicizing the finding in order to increase the chances of finding the owner. A rationale for this law has been explained as follows: "The Abarbanel says that the act of returning an object will cause people to feel compassion and consideration for fellow human beings. People will feel better about one another in general, and this feeling will spread to all aspects of man's relationship to man."[10] Parenthetically, this applies also to finding objects belonging to a non-Jew.

Standing by Idly

A Jew must be a responsible citizen and may not stand by idly and do nothing when some evil action or crime is being committed. He or she has a legal responsibility to help save the person in trouble – for example, a person drowning. At the extreme, a Jew is responsible to intervene to prevent the death of another even if it requires killing the potential killer. In this same category, a person who has information that

10 Amsel, *Jewish Encyclopedia*, 240.

could help another and withholds it is guilty for not providing it.

Religious Duties

Arevut is highly expressed in the domain of performance of religious commandments: the most obvious is the very notion of the quorum or "minyan" required for public prayer. In Jewish law public prayer has a different status from individual prayer. Public prayer is always received, while individual prayer is answered based on individual merit. Also, because much of the prayer text is written in the plural, each person prays for the welfare of the community. Thus public prayer reinforces the lateral bonds between individuals.

Also public prayer involves the appointment of a prayer leader as the representative of the assembly, called the *shaliah tzibbur* (literally, "messenger of the public"). When that person performs a required reading, it is done on behalf of each person and is as if each person had performed it. This type of representation can also occur between two individuals where one person may read for another who is unable. This too is based on the notion of mutual responsibility.

Forgiveness from the Wronged Party

The principal benefit of Yom Kippur, which is obtaining forgiveness for one's sins, is withheld when it comes to a wrong done to another person. That wrong can only be resolved between the two individuals, with the wronged party providing forgiveness. The wrongdoer cannot expect God to provide the forgiveness that can come only from the person who was wronged. In the same context, any lingering hatred or feelings of revenge or grudge must be resolved before Yom Kippur. As a result, that day provides an exceptional opportunity for conflict resolution, elimination of hatred through sincere forgiveness, reconciliation, and peacemaking between Jews.

Purim

In the year 355 BCE,[11] the whole Jewish people were in exile in Persia and faced with extinction after Haman (the king's confidant) had obtained a legal decree to exterminate the Jews. In making his case, he pointed out that the Jews of the empire were scattered and fragmented, and he questioned their allegiance. His plan was on the verge of being executed, but there was one ray of hope for the Jews: unbeknown to Haman, the queen, Esther, was Jewish. She intervened on behalf of her people precisely by ordering that all Jews be gathered to face their sense of common destiny through communal fasting and prayer. When she succeeded in saving her nation, the sages instituted permanent legislation aimed at unifying Jews. On each holiday of Purim, Jews express their *arevut* by giving to the poor and needy (at least a single gift to two poor people) and sending portions of food (at least two) to a friend. The stated purpose is to show love and companionship and promote friendship among Jews.

Mourning during the Omer

Another striking example of the importance given by our sages to *arevut* is illustrated by the legislation of a mourning period during the Omer, the seven weeks separating the holidays of Passover (Pessah) and the Feast of Weeks (Shavuot). Traveling from Pessah to Shavuot, the Jewish calendar moves from physical to spiritual freedom, and this should have been a period of joy in anticipation of reexperiencing the Torah revelation on Shavuot. Yet, the sages turned this period into one of national mourning during which weddings and similar celebrations are suspended: the Jewish people mourn the premature death of twenty-four thousand students of Rabbi Akiva.

---

11   Some Jewish historians date it at 357 BCE.

Rabbi Akiva was an exceptional teacher and his twenty-four thousand students represented the future of the Oral Law. The Talmud attributes their death to the fact that they were deficient in proper respect toward each other. The relationship between the fault of not dealing respectfully with each other and the punishment of untimely death is articulated as follows by Rabbi Aryeh Kaplan:

> During this period of preparation for receiving the Torah, they should have put aside any differences – no matter how minute – that may have existed between them; they should have lived in perfect harmony and unity. Since they maintained their so-called rivalries, even during this period, they were punished precisely during these crucial weeks.... The very act of receiving the Torah required total unity on the part of the Jews. Without such unity, our acceptance of the Torah cannot be complete. And without the Torah, we are nothing.[12]

As mentioned in the previous chapter, this is another example of the fact that discord and hatred among Jews is not simply a private affair, but has national repercussions.

Ninth of Av

The ninth day of the Hebrew month of Av is the saddest day of the yearly calendar.[13] It was legislated as a day of national mourning because of the numerous calamities that befell the Jews on that day throughout their history. In the three sections below, we review the three tragedies that took place on the ninth day of Av in the year 70 CE (the destruction of the Holy Temple, the destruction of Jerusalem, and the beginning of

---

12 Aryeh Kaplan, "The Omer," in *Seasons of the Soul: Religious, Historical, and Philosophical Perspectives on the Jewish Year and Its Milestones*, ed. Rabbi Nisson Wolpin (New York: Mesorah Publications, 1981), 229.

13 For a complete account, consult Kaplan, *The Story of Tisha B'Av*.

the 1,878-year exile from the Land of Israel) from the perspective of baseless hatred.

The Destruction of the Holy Temple. The very existence of the Temple of Jerusalem was predicated on the unity of the Jewish people. When the Land of Israel was divided among the twelve tribes, it was established that the Temple Mount would be divided such that the eastern part of the Temple would be part of the land of the tribe of Judah while the western part would be in the portion of Benjamin. In fact, this design had deep historical roots: it dates back to the blessings that Jacob gave to his children prior to his death.[14]

This sharing of the Temple between Judah and Benjamin had a specific meaning: it sealed the unity of the Jewish people according to the commitment that Judah made to give his life for his brother Benjamin. As we learned in the previous chapter, with that action Judah originated the uniquely Jewish principle of *arevut*. The sharing arrangement between the tribes of Judah and Benjamin was supposed to remind all Jews that access to the Temple was a privilege based on their responsibility toward each other. When baseless hatred spread and destroyed the unity among Jews, the Temple no longer had a reason to exist.

The Destruction of Jerusalem. It should be noted that the city of Jerusalem is not mentioned by its current name in the Torah and there are several reasons for this fact. However, Jerusalem is referred to on multiple occasions, because of its future central role in the life of the Jewish people in the Land of Israel. The nature of that pivotal role can be derived from the formula "the chosen place from all your tribes" (Deuteronomy 12:5). This designation meant that Jerusalem was the point of unification of all the tribes. This theme is found explicitly in Psalm 122: "Yerushalayim, built as a city that fosters togetherness: There

14 Genesis 49:1–28.

the tribes went up, the tribes of God.... For the sake of my brethren and companions, I will say, 'Peace be with you.'"

This principle was followed by King David when he founded Jerusalem. When he bought the city of Jerusalem for six hundred gold shekels, he collected fifty shekels from each of the twelve tribes such that Jerusalem became the common property of all the tribes of Israel. As explained by Rabbi Aryeh Kaplan: "As one place common to all, it had a strong effect in uniting the tribes."[15] We should remember that unity among tribes is not possible if individual Jews within each tribe are disunited. Therefore, when baseless hatred destroyed the unity of the tribes, Jerusalem had no reason to exist.

The Beginning of the Exile. As indicated in the last three chapters, hatred creates psychological and physical distances between individuals. A person who hates feels distant from his or her object of hate and has practically "exiled" that person. When hatred is reciprocal between two persons, they avoid being in the same place and cannot stand the sight of each other.

When the generation of the Second Temple allowed hatred to spread, they created large psychological distances among themselves. They were so separated from each other that they were in exile even while they lived in the same land. Consequently, there was no need for them to live close to each other. In fact, it was perhaps painful for them to be so close to each other and they needed more space. So, why not spread over the whole planet?

When they ceased being a united people, they no longer needed the Land of Israel and it was taken away from them. The Land of Israel was promised and given to a people, not to a group of individuals. When the

---

15   Aryeh Kaplan, *Jerusalem: The Eye of the Universe* (New York: NCSY/UOJC, 1976), 67.

Jews do not form one people, they do not need the land!

Thus, when the Jews were no longer united they lost their three symbols of national unity: the Temple, Jerusalem, and the Land of Israel.

Conclusion

Arevut constitutes the commitment to mutual responsibility that must exist among Jews. Baseless hatred destroys *arevut* because it destroys the basic capacity of empathy among human beings. In this chapter, we described how *arevut* was officially incorporated into the infrastructure of the Jewish people at the covenant at Sinai, during the formative years of the Jewish people under the leadership of Moses and when the Jewish people entered the Land of Israel. Then we saw how it was broadly and permanently integrated into Jewish law (social laws, religious laws, and commemorations).

It was also suggested that when baseless hatred becomes rampant and the Jews turn from being one people into a group of individuals, they no longer need (or deserve) the Land of Israel and they are exiled. This reasoning was applied to the events that preceded the year 70 CE, the beginning of the long exile. Since 1948, a new question has arisen: Does this hatred-exile logic work in the opposite direction? If the Jews are able to end their physical exile as they did in 1948, what does it say about the status of baseless hatred? If hatred causes exile, does the end of exile spell the end of baseless hatred? Or does the persistence of the spiritual exile in the continued absence of the Holy Temple indicate that baseless hatred is still with us?

Part 2

Israel and the Jews

5

The 1948 Question: Two Generations

The creation of the State of Israel compels us to address one fundamental question: Does the baseless hatred-exile relationship work in reverse, i.e., did the end of the long physical exile spell the end of baseless hatred among Jews? If not, how did it impact it? In 1948 the Jews were able to establish the first Jewish government in their homeland in 1,878 years, and with Jewish control of the land, Jewish habitation in the land increased once again to a critical mass after nearly two thousand years of very minimal physical presence. What happened then to baseless hatred in the midst of the Jews assembled in Israel?

Answering this question is a very complex endeavor for the following reason: any analysis of the state of relationships among Jews in their new state must take into consideration the relationship of Israel with the outside world. It is practically impossible to assess intra-Jewish relations in isolation in a state faced with five wars in its first twenty-five years of existence, starting with the War of Independence the day after the Proclamation of Independence. But what emerges from this attempt to analyze the state of *arevut* in Israel is a strange Israeli behavior: the reaction to outside opposition or hatred can take two opposite forms. If it is interpreted as existential, it can become a unifying factor. This is what Rabbi Jonathan Sacks refers to as "a unity imposed, as it were, from outside,"[1] and this is essentially what occurred during the first three decades of the life of the modern State of Israel.

A contrary or reverse behavior took place during the second three decades, where external opposition was absorbed and internalized in ways that resulted in dysfunctional divisiveness. This chapter analyzes key events in the first sixty-two years of the State of Israel (1948–2010) viewed through the lenses of *arevut* and baseless hatred. This analysis is divided into two periods of three decades.

1948–1979: The First Three Decades

As the State of Israel arose in 1948, baseless hatred was not on the national agenda. The new state had existential challenges, and its focus was on the essentials, on survival. However, the very process of building a country and its institutions contributed to a spirit of sharing a common goal.

National Home

In his famous declaration on November 2, 1917, Arthur James Balfour addressed the establishment of a "national home" for the Jewish people. We know that he and the other members of the British government were careful about words and their political implications. But, for complex

---

1 Sacks, *One People*, viii.

and unexplained reasons, they saw fit to use the same language that the founders of the Zionist movement had used (First Zionist Congress, Basel, 1897).

Over the years, Herzl had pleaded for a national home because the Jews needed a place where they could live in safety. Since the Jews were not welcomed in other lands, it became obvious that a Jewish home had to be a state, if Jews were to control their destiny. Herzl had pointed out that, for centuries, Jews had tried hard to be someone else, to adopt the identities of their environments, but to no avail. Therefore, in their home, they would have the opportunity to be who they truly are. Home is where people are themselves. Home is where Jews were supposed to form a people.

Herzl was enamored with the notion of peoplehood, of all Jews assembled forming one entity. The main objective was that Jews would no longer be at the mercy of others and would be able to control their destiny. They would no longer be "politically impotent." As Israel's first president, David Ben-Gurion, was to say: "Since 73 B.C.E., the Wandering Jew has been a stereotype. But never for those who remained or returned here. In the Land of Israel there is no such thing. This is home. And at home the Jew, like people everywhere, digs his soil, builds his abode, fights to defend every inch of the ground he cherishes so highly."[2]

The State of Israel did just what Herzl had dreamed of: it offered Jews the opportunity to redefine the notion of a Jewish entity and of Jewish unity in multiple ways, for the first time in almost two thousand years. This notion of home is critical in the historical context of the hatred-*arevut* paradigm because it is always "at home" that the phenomenon of hatred acquires unique proportions (see below and in chapter 9).

---

2 David Ben-Gurion, *Memoirs* (Cleveland: The World Publishing Company, 1970), 115.

The new state offered personal safety in terms of protection from arbitrary antisemitic measures, but the inhabitants still had to face enemies (see below).

Immigration

In 1948, the Jewish population of Israel was only 630,000 – less than that of any major city in the rest of the world. If the new state did not achieve a population of at least one million very rapidly, it would not obtain respectability in the world community, and it would remain vulnerable to the armies of the surrounding countries. However, neither previous Jewish history nor the founders of the Zionist movement provided a mechanism to uproot Jews from different countries all at once. The leaders wondered how they could entice millions of Jews to immigrate to a country with a minimal infrastructure. Here also, a combination of improbable events achieved the unexpected.

The first immigrants arrived from refugee camps in Europe and from camps in Cyprus that held Jews trying to reach Israel (illegally) during the British Mandate. Within one decade, a large inflow of Jews from Yemen, Iraq, Libya, Morocco, Algeria, Tunisia, Iran, Egypt, Syria, and Afghanistan saved the day. Within the first decade, the 630,000 Israelis had welcomed 900,000 new immigrants (of whom 684,000 had come in the first three years). Such a mass of newcomers had economic, social, and cultural needs. The efforts to settle them were so overwhelming that social tensions became unavoidable. There was an immediate demand for housing, public schools, a health system, and hospitals, at the same time that military spending had to be maximized. Just to take one example, housing had to be in reception camps with transition housing and temporary resettlement. Until today, immigrants recall the dreary and depressing accommodations and the hardships they had to endure.

Compared to those pressing issues, it seemed that baseless hatred was not among the priorities of the new state. Yet, the building of basic institutions for the new state (a national home, a unifying modern language, military service, the adoption of a state calendar based upon the millennia-old Jewish calendar) created a new Jewish people as had never existed for nineteen centuries.

Language

Even before the state was created, it was decided that Hebrew was going to be the official language. In Israel, the Hebrew language came back to life. "We opted," remembered David Ben-Gurion, "for our natural speech, the language of our inheritance, our sovereignty and our association with this part of the world."[3] *Ulpanim* (language learning centers) where Hebrew was taught became a national industry. Israelis began to use a new language which was an old language and most importantly, it was their own language.

Many think that it is unprecedented to have a language die and be revived after nineteen centuries. But Hebrew had never died. It had been kept alive and well by the rabbis of all the Diaspora communities, who had an ongoing need to communicate to address the issues of Jewish law that arose in their communities. They were in different countries with different languages. The rabbis wrote in Hebrew and communicated the most mundane of situations or the most esoteric notions through a system of *she'elot* and *teshuvot*, questions and answers. Communication continued uninterrupted for centuries. As one historian of Hebrew pointed out: "It was the language of prayer, study, reading the Torah, and correspondence. Above all it was used as the language of a tremendously rich literature of law, theology, philosophy, science, medicine, astronomy,

3 Ibid., 130.

poetry, grammar and other fields of human knowledge."[4] This is how the dispersed Jewish people were able to communicate as if they were one unit. They preserved not just vocabulary but also the complex rules of grammar and the methodology to fabricate new words based on existing roots. That enabled the impassioned linguistic pioneer Eliezer Ben-Yehudah (and his organization Va'ad ha-Lashon ha-Ivrit, later Academy of the Hebrew Language) to succeed in meeting the needs of the new state.

Reestablishing Hebrew as the only currency of communication on a national scale was an amazing feat of the State of Israel. A common language provided a framework of uniqueness and unity. Having their own language for everyday interactions created a unique wavelength of communication, shared by no one else. They understood each other better because the words they used had well-established "Jewish" meanings. Although mutual responsibility or *arevut* was not on the national agenda per se, having a common language provided the type of framework needed to weaken inter-individual animosity and strengthen connections between Jews as members of the same nation, people, and family. Indeed there is ample evidence that this occurred, because a unique characteristic of the Israeli culture is its informality. Until today, Israelis who have never seen each other are able to connect on an intimate level when they speak in Hebrew.

Calendar and Holidays

The creation of the state offered other opportunities to promote unity among Jews. First there was the adoption of the Shabbat as the national day of rest and the Jewish holidays as official holidays. This new calendar contributed to the sense of identity of the new Israelis because

---

4   Edward Horowitz, *How the Hebrew Language Grew* (Jersey City, NJ: Ktav, 1960), 6.

it was based on authentically Jewish traditions. There was the flag and the national anthem. Also, critical days like Yom Hazikaron and Yom Ha'atzmaut were created. On Yom Hazikaron, the day of remembrance, Israelis remember the soldiers they lost in all their wars. This is a unique day in the yearly calendar: it is somber but it unites all families who have sacrificed children or siblings in the prime of their lives. Yom Ha'atzmaut, the day of independence, is an equivalent of America's July 4 on which Israelis celebrate their new state and its accomplishments. Recently, the Knesset voted to establish the tenth day of the month of Iyar, the birthday of Theodor Herzl, as a day of celebration to honor his contributions as the founder of modern political Zionism.

Army Service

From its first day of existence, the state had to organize its defense. The new government had no official army, just independent private fighting units that were not coordinated. Unification took place through the creation of the Israel Defense Forces (IDF), composed mostly of civilians (today the Israeli army has 140,000 full-time troops versus three times as many reservists who serve for at least one month per year). All Israelis were expected to participate.

On a personal and national level, the Israeli army was a potent unifying force because it assembled and taught Jews from the many different communities, with differences in ethnicity, culture, tradition, and approach to Judaism. The IDF handled each new wave of immigrants and helped them adapt to their new country. It created a sense of purpose and common destiny. Out of each war or military operation came reports of soldiers displaying acts of heroism and giving their lives for others. Throughout Israel's history, these Jews reenacted the original and historical Judah-*arevut* principle of putting one's life at risk to save one's brother or sister. Some have resented the non-participation of much of

Israel's most religious population in the armed services, while others have pointed out that just as Issachar and Zebulun divided spiritual and material responsibilities, so too those who dedicate their lives to Torah and *mitzvot* (the commandments of Jewish law) are doing their part in the defense of the country in the spiritual realm.

As Caroline Glick wrote for the *Jerusalem Post*: "Israelis are among the most patriotic citizens of the world. Our patriotism is expressed in the high level of volunteerism in all age groups. In the recent war [the Second Lebanon War of 2006], tens of thousands of reservists willingly left their families and jobs to take up arms and defend the country, and hundreds of thousands of Israelis volunteered to help our one million brothers and sisters whose homes were targeted by rockets, missiles and mortars."[5]

Wars

From 1948 to 1979, Israelis had to fight five wars: the War of Independence (1947–1948), the Suez Campaign (1956), and the Six-Day War (1967), followed by the War of Attrition (1968–1970) and the Yom Kippur War (1973). The first war, the War of Independence, began the morning after Ben-Gurion read the Declaration of Independence: the Egyptians managed to bomb Tel Aviv while the armies of Transjordan, Lebanon, Syria, and Iraq invaded.

These wars had multiple effects on Israeli society. The first four wars helped formulate the image of the new Jew as a warrior who was courageous and victorious. That was particularly the case of the Six-Day War. That war had a unique impact because, in a short time, encircled Israeli forces managed to destroy the Egyptian air force and conquer the

---

5 Caroline B. Glick, *Shackled Warrior: Israel and the Global Jihad* (Jerusalem: Gefen Publishing House, 2008), 425.

Sinai Peninsula, as well as conquer the Golan Heights and the West Bank. Most importantly they liberated Jerusalem. The emotions associated with that event were close to euphoric and sustained Israelis for six years until the next war. The pictures of the first Israeli soldiers and shofar blowing at the Western Wall – the last remaining physical remnant of the Holy Temple and therefore the holiest site to Judaism, from which Jews had been barred since the Jordanian takeover of the Old City of Jerusalem in the 1948 War of Independence – made instant history.

We saw at the end of the previous chapter that, historically, Jerusalem functioned as the point of unification of all the tribes, "built as a city that fosters togetherness" (Psalm 122), as one place common to all. This actually happened in 1967 and in the following years. Throngs of Israelis walked to the Western Wall. Those who lived in Israel at the time speak about the holiday of Shavuot which fell in the week following the recapture of the Old City: more than 250,000 Jews came to the Western Wall that day, recreating the atmosphere of the three main religious holidays (Pessah, Shavuot, Sukkot) during the period of the holy Temple.

Everyone in Israel was affected. The symbolism associated with Jerusalem as the state capital contributed immensely to unifying Israeli society. The reunification of Jerusalem reverberated and affected Jews all over the world. This is how it was described by Natan Sharansky:

> Then, in six dramatic days, everything changed for us. The call that went up from Jerusalem, "The Temple Mount is in our hand" penetrated the Iron Curtain and forged an almost mystic link with our people. And while we had no idea what the Temple Mount was, we did know that the fact that it was in our hands had won us respect. Like a cry from our distant past, it told us that we were no

longer displaced and isolated. We belonged to something even if we did not know what or why.[6]

That euphoria lasted until October 6, 1973, when Egypt and Syria launched a coordinated surprise attack. In order to reverse initial enemy gains, the Israeli forces had to fight until October 24 and lose 2,569 men and women (as well as suffer 7,500 wounded and 301 prisoners). The illusion of invulnerability was forever gone.

Interestingly, those Israeli losses allowed Egyptian president Anwar Sadat to publicly declare victory in Egypt. Simultaneously, he knew that he had lost the Sinai Peninsula and wanted to recapture it at any price. This led to his taking, four years later, the unprecedented step of visiting Jerusalem and making his historic address at the Knesset (Israeli parliament). And from this in turn came the peace negotiations that resulted in the Camp David Accords in September 1978 and the Israel-Egypt peace treaty the following year.

Assessment at the End of the First Three Decades

If one were to make a global assessment at the end of the first three decades, it would be that the Zionist dream had succeeded to a significant extent. Multiple reasons and hypotheses can be proposed to explain that success. One of them is that its founders and pioneers (Herzl, Ben-Gurion, Rabbi Abraham Isaac Kook), whatever their particular orientation, all shared the central goal of reuniting the Jewish people with its land. After thirty years of existence, the new State of Israel had laid a firm foundation for the future of the Jewish people, which was an unprecedented achievement in the context of the preceding nineteen centuries of Jewish history.

Even though the issue of baseless hatred per se had not been officially on

---

6   Natan Sharansky, "The Political Legacy of Theodor Herzl," *Azure* 21 (2005): 87.

the state's agenda, most of the state institutions enhanced the potential for the development of *arevut* on a large scale. There were a number of challenges and unresolved issues that had become apparent, but most of them were expected. For example, the result of successful immigration was that Israel was populated by Jews who looked different, had different cultures, felt differently about issues, spoke different languages, and had different degrees of religiosity. This new matrix of disparate Jews presented serious challenges with respect to the issue of unity and *arevut*. Israel had in fact been called one nation made of several "tribes." At the macroscopic level there are Ashkenazim, Mizrahim, and Sephardim. Ashkenazim are divided into various groups of Hasidim, Mitnagdim, etc. Then each of these groups subdivided itself into individual countries of origin and sometimes even further.

Superimposed on this "melting pot" issue was the "religious-secular divide," which manifested itself in many ways. Among other points of contention, some of these included obvious visible manifestations such as type and color of clothing, degree of modesty, and hair and head covering. These external appearances sometimes created friction, particularly when different Jews shared common public transportation. Even private transportation became an issue on the Shabbat day of rest in certain areas. Some difficult religion-related issues were addressed with some degree of success during the first three decades, such as the availability of kosher food in public institutions (army, hospitals) and hotels. But many others were left unattended, particularly the status of *agunot* (divorcees who have not received a proper Jewish divorce document), the conversion process (who is a Jew), and exemption from military service.

The most significant aspect of the first three decades of the State of Israel was that its external political issues were in essence existential and therefore to a large extent had a unifying effect on the Israeli population.

Although there were certainly divisions among political parties, the Israeli people knew that the five wars (the War of Independence, Suez Campaign, Six-Day War, War of Attrition, and the Yom Kippur War) were unequivocally life-threatening for the state and for every individual. Soldiers and those who volunteered were convinced that they were confronting the enemy to protect their families and homes. That situation changed drastically during the second three decades.

1980–2010: The Second Three Decades

Understanding the evolution of external threats to Israel and their interpretation within Israeli society is critical to addressing the state of present-day divisiveness. In these second thirty years, at least four new simultaneous currents emerged:

1. The nature of external threats changed.
2. The pursuit of peace became a national obsession – and failed.
3. The fire of the Zionist dream was not sustained among a new generation of Israelis.
4. Western countries ended their traditional support of Israel.

By 2010, there was a feeling among Israeli society that Israel had to restart its relationships with the outside world. This led to new existential issues.

Evolution of External Threats

Taking a retrospective vantage point, we can say that in the first three decades, there was a sort of synergy between the internal focus of building a state and the defense efforts to survive external threats. Internally, several of the new state's institutions (language, army, calendar, national education) served to unify Jews and create a new society. Externally, Israel was fighting traditional wars against foreign armies (Egypt, Syria, Jordan) and foreign governments. Any failure in those wars – notably in the cases of the War of Independence, the Six-Day War, or the Yom Kippur War – could have resulted in the annihilation of the state. For example, books about the Six-Day War describe the *hamtanah* (waiting period) preceding the war, during which the uncertainty about the outcome united the nation in an unprecedented way.

During the second thirty years, the nature of external threats to Israel changed in ways that could not have been imagined.

Israelis were accustomed to American support, which was expressed politically and financially and was obvious to the world. Anwar Sadat, president of Egypt, had complained about it: "The glasses the United States is wearing on its eyes are entirely Zionist glasses, completely blind to everything except what Israel wants."[7] But in the last twenty years, Israelis experienced something odd: the direct involvement of the United States in 1991 (Operation Desert Storm) and 2003 (Iraq War) to destroy a vocal enemy of Israel without any involvement by Israel's military. This departure from the previous American policy of more distant political and financial support to a more direct policy of military involvement in the region created a new reality that posed some challenges for Israel.

Also, unlike the Six-Day and Yom Kippur Wars, Israel's wars were now military campaigns (the two Lebanon wars, Operation Cast Lead in Gaza) where soldiers were no longer fighting foreign armies but bands of terrorists hidden among civilians. Even the first intifada, which was not viewed as seriously threatening, became a disproportionately troubling issue. Israeli politician Yossi Beilin has observed: "The intifada

---

7 Mitchell G. Bard, *Myths and Facts: A Guide to the Arab-Israeli Conflict* (Chevy Chase, MD: American Israeli Cooperative Enterprise, 2006), 69.

did not pose an existential threat to Israel, but it constituted a continuing nuisance, aggravated the sense of personal insecurity and seriously harmed Israel's image in the world."[8] Yet Israel with all its might did not know how to respond. Beilin continues:

> A debate raged in Israel for many months on whether or not the Defense Minister had explicitly instructed the soldiers to break arms and legs of the Palestinian demonstrators…. There was no one who desired the end of the intifada or sought answers to the intifada more than the Israelis, but the world was not satisfied with this…. The small, sophisticated, moral Israel of the 1950s and 1960s was transformed in the eyes of the young generation of television viewers from David into Goliath, while the stone throwers became the modern-day Davids.[9]

This new type of threat to Israel, which, unlike previous ones, was not existential, somehow fueled internal dissension. Young Israelis, even those serving in the IDF, began to have second thoughts because they did not consider these campaigns to be essential self-defense. Even the targeted assassinations of terrorists were internally criticized. The government of Israel was accused of "disproportionate use of force" and killing women and children, and some of the younger Israelis believed those accusations.

Fruitless Pursuit of Peace

In this second thirty-year period, one example of the role of external factors on the internal well-being of Israeli society was the Oslo peace process. The peace process captured the minds of all Israelis, to the point of obsession. Typical of the mood of the day was this commentary from

---

8 Yossi Beilin, *Israel: A Concise Political History* (New York: St. Martin's, 1992), 47.

9 Ibid., 48–49.

Shimon Peres: "A rare opportunity to create a new Golden Age in the Middle East has arisen after the Gulf War. We can begin today by taking the first steps across the bridge of mutual cooperation and understanding among Middle East peoples."[10]

Those present among the small group of Israeli, Palestinian, and Norwegian delegates in Oslo retell the emotions they felt staying up all night to initial the final documents on August 20, 1993. The PLO had expressed its willingness to officially recognize Israel's right to exist in peace, therefore renouncing the use of terrorism. The PLO representatives had also agreed to eradicate some thirty-three articles in the Palestinian National Covenant that referred to the destruction of Israel. Israelis were allowed to dream; there was a three-step program of cooperation: binational or multinational projects, international consortiums, and regional community policy.

The Israeli government had taken a big chance in dealing with Yasser Arafat. The Israeli population was taken through ups and downs all carefully modulated by Arafat, extremely skilled at deceptive strategies and double-talk. His true intent was hidden inside the "phased struggle" formula, coined by him to weather the setbacks of the 1973 Yom Kippur War and the 1977 visit to Jerusalem of Egyptian president Anwar Sadat. He used the phased struggle formula when speaking to Palestinian Arabs. Western countries were taken by Arafat's speeches at the United Nations and during the so-called 1991 Madrid Peace Conference. The deception included the 1993 Arafat-Rabin letters of mutual recognition renouncing the use of terrorism. It took the West and the Israeli public a long time to understand that Arafat was no Sadat.

Israelis experienced moments full of hope, like the memorable

---

10 Shimon Peres with Arye Naor, *The New Middle East* (New York: Henry Holt and Company, 1993), cover.

September 13, 1993, ceremony on the White House lawn when Prime Minister Yitzhak Rabin shook hands with Yasser Arafat under the eye of President Bill Clinton acting as host and witness. Western countries chased Arafat for years to have him redraft the PNA/PLO charter to expunge the language pertaining to the destruction of Israel, but to no avail. US president Bill Clinton even came to Gaza in person to obtain a hand vote, but a copy of the new draft renouncing Israel's destruction was never issued. It was President Clinton's determination and boundless investment of goodwill (shared by most Israelis) that began to reveal Arafat's true intentions in the summer of 2000 at Camp David.

Some of the reported exchanges between the two men shed some light. Clinton said to Arafat: "If the Israelis can make compromises and you can't, I should go home. You have been here 14 days and said no to everything. These things will have consequences. Failure will end the peace process."[11] And, reports Mitchell Bard, "In his last conversation with President Clinton, Arafat told the President that he was 'a great man.' Clinton responded, 'The hell I am. I'm a colossal failure, and you made me one.'"[12]

Following the failure of the Camp David negotiations, the second intifada started. The communications minister of the PLO later acknowledged that the outbreak of the intifada was at the request of Arafat as part of his global strategy. These events had catastrophic consequences on the unity of Israeli society because they had struggled to arrive at making serious concessions to the PLO. One segment of Israeli society clearly recognized that the Palestinian position was not about land or configuration of their state but strictly about Jews not having any piece of land as a sovereign state.

---

11   Bard, *Myths and Facts*, 262.

12   Ibid., 247.

Perception of Successive Failures

When we try to tally the key events in this period, we find that they add up to a series of societal upheavals: the First (1982–2000) and Second (2006) Lebanon Wars; the two intifadas of 1987–1992 and 2000–2005 (the latter following the failure of the Camp David summit). In the summer of 2005, the tragic expulsion of Jews from Gush Katif in Gaza was a traumatic event for Israeli society. The population included eight thousand Jews, some of whom had lived there since 1968. From what had been before their presence there a barren strip of land, they had developed a very successful economy that accounted for 15 percent of the agricultural exports of the state. They had endured attacks during the first and second intifadas. They had served the state as a "buffer zone." In the end, as religious Zionists, they were labeled as "settlers" and "land grabbers" and forcibly evicted by the Israeli army.

The Israeli army had the decency to leave public buildings, greenhouses, and synagogues intact. As soon as the army withdrew, the Gush Katif residents and the rest of the Israeli public were subjected to images of Palestinian Arabs ransacking all that had been left intact, including holy sites. The Gush Katif episode left permanent scars on Israeli society. The descriptions of the residents in the Israeli press had tragic consequences because they invited virulent criticism in the world press. The expulsion from Gush Katif and withdrawal from Gaza was followed by the violent Hamas takeover of the Gaza Strip in 2007. The "democratically" elected Hamas began to attack the Israeli city of Sderot with daily launches of rockets and missiles, which then led to Operation Cast Lead in the final days of 2008 and first days of 2009. That operation unleashed worldwide criticism of Israel, although it was undertaken purely to put an end to more than two years of shelling of innocent Israeli civilians from within Gaza.

Beginning with the Oslo peace process, this series of failures had profound consequences on several segments of Israeli society, including its enlightened lay leadership, academia, journalists, and writers. Several academic leaders took positions and actions that were unprecedented even among the most secular segments of society because they crossed the line in their "post-Zionist" – or some would say "anti-Zionist" or even "anti-Israel" – attitudes. This is how it was expressed in an editorial piece by Caroline Glick from December 2003:

> It is an open secret that many of the most prominent Israeli academics and professors are also identified with the radical leftist fringes of the Israeli political spectrum. The Hebrew University's Political Science Department was dominated for years by the leaders of Peace Now. Tel Aviv University's Social Science and Humanities Faculties are the professional home of some of the leaders of the even more radical Ta'ayush and Yesh Gvul organizations.
>
> Israeli professors have signed petitions calling for boycotts of Israeli goods. Some have even supported the boycott of Israeli academics by foreign universities and academic publications. Israel Radio reported this week that the letter written by 13 reservists from the elite Sayeret Matkal commando unit in which they announced their refusal to serve in the territories was written for them by a Tel Aviv university professor."[13]

In the same editorial, the author gives the example of a Tel Aviv University law professor who "published a policy paper at USC where he argues that Israel's territorial claims to land it secured during the 1948–49 War of Independence are no different from its claim to land secured in the 1967 Six-Day War. In his view both are illegitimate."[14] This degree of dissent had crossed a dangerous internal line.

---

13 Glick, *Shackled Warrior*, 306.

14 Ibid., 307.

Confusion of the Younger Generation

As described above, the Zionist dream was essentially realized in the first three decades of the state's existence. In the second three decades, Israeli society faced the challenge of maintaining the original spirit and dedication of the Zionist founders. That meant transferring it from one generation to the next. But how does one transfer a dream? Interestingly, the Zionist philosophy that propelled Jews from 1890 to 1948 did not include a recipe for its own continuity. Once the primary objective was achieved and a state was established, the early Zionists had no method to convince new generations to follow in their footsteps, to love and cultivate the land.

By the year 2000, most of the founders of the state had died. Their achievements were now part of history. Their accomplishments could not continue to be viewed as miracles by the next two generations. The state and its institutions were taken for granted by the younger generations who were born into them. Specifically, children were born who did not value the kibbutz life of their parents and who had minimal ties with the foundations of Jewishness. Their parents were the secularists who lead the Zionist movement and had themselves broken with the traditions of their fathers and mothers. Zionist leaders openly distanced themselves from the image of the Diaspora Jew and did not believe in religious traditions. Also, for them, Israel was a state while Judaism was a religion, and a state was distinct from religion. They had inherited the state-religion distinction from the struggles of the various European states with Christianity, as expressed by Yoram Hazony: "With respect to Christianity,…the modern state was forged in the midst of a rebellion against Catholicism." He explains that thinkers such as Hobbes and Locke fought against the ability of "a single man sitting in Italy" to

> put an end to discussion about public good in England by saying
> that he had read Scripture and was in possession of miraculous

knowledge, so that no further thought would be required. In Christendom, this understanding of Scripture as a source of present miraculous knowledge meant not the advancement of inquiry into the public good but its suppression. And the struggle to free public discourse from the shackles imposed on it by this kind of religion really is an important part of the heritage of the Western state.[15]

Although the early Zionists had adopted this dichotomous state-religion perspective, Hazony explains that Judaism, on the other hand, had dealt with such concerns and had a completely different approach to societal issues: "Reasoning concerning what will bring the public good is not proscribed by Jewish religion, but required by it." However, the Zionist leaders were highly suspicious of any religion. They believed in a new Sabra Jew who was a fighter and in charge of his or her own destiny. They had no interest in any "traditional" Jewish content of the educational system. Zionism was a dream about the creation of a Jewish home; it was for adult consumption and had not dealt with the complexities of a child's identity or the issue of intergenerational transmission, particularly once the home was established.

Israeli children born in the period 1980–1990 had neither memories of the torments of living in the Diaspora nor the initial euphoria of Jewish sovereignty that sustained Israelis in the 1950s and 1960s. Their education did not have a Jewish content, and Zionism was part of the early (and to them ancient) history of their state. With them Zionism had somehow lost its unifying magic, and the links uniting Jews had been seriously weakened. It became clear that the commitment required to maintain the state as Jewish and its population united is not pre-programmed in Jewish genes. Furthermore, the concept that Jewish might was the solution to Jewish problems was gradually failing.

---

15   Yoram Hazony, "Judaism and the Modern State," *Azure* 21 (2005): 33.

Assessment at the End of the Second Three Decades

These decades turned out to be traumatic and transformative for Israeli society. There were a series of objective reasons. Every effort invested by Israelis in the peace process with Palestinian Arabs had failed. More recently, additional failures included the Gaza withdrawal followed by the emergence of Hamas, the Second Lebanon War followed by the strengthening of Hezbollah with the help of Syria and Iran. Then, Iran joined the fray with overt calls for the annihilation of the State of Israel through the use of nuclear weapons (see chapter 6). A particular turning point was the realization that most Western countries, including the United States, had decided to end their traditional support of Israel (see chapter 7). Furthermore, its legality came under attack, not just by its traditional enemies (chapter 6), but by a chorus of nations (chapter 7). The shadow of the Holocaust had vanished for good.

Despite Israel's military strength and its success in the fields of computing, communications, and biotechnology, its line of credit with the world had somehow run out. All of a sudden, it seemed to Israelis as if their country had accomplished little in sixty years. Why? Because the external difficulties faced by Israel had somehow been amplified by internal dissention and absorbed internally. Whatever gain in *arevut* was achieved in the first thirty years did not seem to protect Israeli society from putting its unity at risk. One apparent reason is that, in general, Jews tend to not simply react to each other but to overreact and even become intolerant. Why?

It is not that Jews are not polite or civilized. Rather, it may be because they care about each other's opinions to the point that they feel threatened by differences in attitude. That is an inappropriate response, and it must be understood and addressed because it amounts to intolerance. How can we explain this complex behavior? Could it be that they refuse to admit that individuals who are important to them can think so differently (and, in their minds, erroneously)? Or could it be because they refuse to admit that individuals for whom they have contempt are in fact important to them? Under either hypothesis, overreactions erupt because they "silently" or implicitly care about each other but do not admit it. Even if the basis of this behavior is "silent *arevut*," it is not true *arevut* because it practically results in intolerance and *arevut* is about mutual responsibility.

Another reason why interactions between Jews are unique may be based on the "last Jew" syndrome. Throughout their history, Jews struggled to survive and young Jews were taught that the survival of the whole Jewish people depended on them. As a result, each Jew tends to behave as if he or she must be capable of guaranteeing the survival of the Jewish people, as if all other Jews were nonexistent: when a Jew behaves as the last survivor, he or she feels very strongly about his or her opinions and positions and may become intolerant.

Throughout their history, long before the creation of the State of Israel, Jews were accustomed to differences in opinions; this has been called "the dignity of dissent."[16] But sometimes, intolerant relationships between Jews spring from prejudice and stereotypes, which, as Rush Dozier points out, are easily generated by the primitive neural system: "Us-them prejudice can infect our thinking without our clearly being aware of it."[17] These stereotypes are lethal because they cannot be easily erased and they destroy the cohesiveness of the Jewish people (chapter 9).

These characteristics of Jewish discourse have been recognized and described by many authors: "Nor is there a law of nature that says

---

16 Jonathan Sacks, *Future Tense: Jews, Judaism, and Israel in the Twenty-First Century* (New York: Schocken, 2009), 198.

17 Dozier, *Why We Hate*, 226–27.

that Jews must quarrel with other Jews, frustrate each other's efforts and criticize each other mercilessly, acting as if they were still in the wilderness wondering why they ever left Egypt."[18]

Conclusions

The succession of events of the second thirty years of the State of Israel took a particular toll on the new generation of Israelis born after 1980. Keen observers pointed out that Israelis were for the first time voicing existential questions such as the following, articulated by Daniel Gordis:

> Can Israel survive? Does it deserve to?[19]

> …Israelis have tired of fighting and of sending their children to war, but they have no idea how to settle the conflicts that consume them…. Statehood has revitalized the Jewish people, but the Jews are very unlikely to get another state should this one fail…. Jewish life as we know it would be lost. The regained optimism, vitality, and confidence of the Jewish world would disappear, probably within a generation. Israel's enemies understand that. It is time that the Jews did, too.[20]

At the end of six decades, the status of *arevut* in Israel had deteriorated. The next three chapters address the external opposition faced by Israel and how Israeli and Diaspora Jews should respond by focusing on establishing *arevut*.

---

18 Sacks, *Future Tense*, 6.

19 Daniel Gordis, *Saving Israel: How the Jewish People Can Win a War That May Never End* (Hoboken, NJ: Wiley, 2009), 8.

20 Ibid., 216, 217.

6

The "Palestinian Issue": Land Dispute or Islamist Hatred?

"Hate is uncommonly dangerous because it combines a whole array of behaviors that tend to create and perpetuate animosity and misunderstanding in places such as the Middle East."[1] Fatah, Hamas, and Hezbollah: How are we to understand the basis of their feelings toward Israel? Is it all about a land dispute or is there more to their attitudes? What is politics and what is true hatred? Why do present-day Israelis become divided when confronting this external opposition, instead of uniting as they did in previous conflicts? To address these questions we will trace the evolution of Palestinian Arab attitudes toward Israel over a span of three generations.

---

1 Dozier, *Why We Hate*, 260.

History of the Conflict

Initial Questions

From the beginning of the twentieth century, long before the creation of the State of Israel, Palestinian Arab opposition to the early Zionists seemed to be exclusively about land. The conflict was described as a land dispute between European Jews dedicated to becoming farmers and orange growers, and Palestinian Arabs who viewed them as foreign invaders. Palestinian Arabs feared the reestablishment of a Jewish state, which they viewed as "occupation" of Palestine. In theory, then, all Palestinian Arab animosity toward Israelis would disappear if, somehow, Israelis decided to just pack up and leave.

A few simple questions are in order:

1. How was it possible for "foreign" Zionists to "grab" land that had been under Muslim control for centuries? There was no military invasion. What Zionists had done was to declare at the First Zionist Congress in Basel in 1897 that their aim was to create a home for the Jewish people in Palestine. This raises a second question.

2. How could Herzl and the Zionist Congress set their eyes on someone else's land? Even if they did, it should have had no meaning since they were speaking about land two thousand miles away. This raises the next question.

3. Whose land was it? It was not the Palestinian Arabs'; at the time of the Zionist declaration, Palestine did not exist (in fact the name Palestine is a general term used to describe a broad geographical area but there has never been a sovereign state called Palestine) and its land was part of the Ottoman Empire. Let us note that there were 25,000 Jews and 450,000 Arabs living in the area in 1881, 85,000 Jews and 650,000 Arabs in 1914. Thus at the turn of the century, Jews were a minority.

4. How could a minority of Jews take over a country just because in Basel some Zionists had a dream? All this begs the ultimate question.

5. Why did Palestinian Arabs or other local Muslims not establish a state before Zionists began to dream in Basel? Or between 1948 and 1967, when Egypt and Jordan governed the Gaza Strip and the West Bank, respectively?

6. If the Jews had come at any time and found in place any type of ethnic or national or state-like structure (with a parliament, or flag, or army), the Zionist Congresses' declarations would have been valueless and would have had little or no practical impact.

These questions will be addressed in an attempt to understand the core of the antagonism of Fatah, Hamas, and Hezbollah.

1917–1922: Regional Borders in Flux

World War I gamble. As mentioned in the last chapter, twenty years after the declaration of the First Zionist Congress, the British secretary of state for foreign affairs, Sir Arthur James Balfour, issued on November 2, 1917, the famous declaration in the name of the British government that reproduced the language of establishment of a national home for the Jewish people. It is fundamental for anyone concerned with the Israeli-Palestinian dispute to understand the historical context that surrounded this decision. Without it there would probably not be a State of Israel.

At the time, Palestine was one of many provinces of the Ottoman Empire and just like Iraq, Syria, Jordan, and Lebanon, it had no defined boundaries and was not a political or ethnic entity. For the previous four hundred years, under the Ottomans, what was known as Palestine had no characteristic of a country: "Palestine at the time was not ruled as a united, single, separate administrative entity. It was subdivided into districts, each ruled from a distant capital."[2] There were essentially three distinct zones in Palestine, one ruled from Constantinople, one from Damascus, and the third was itself subdivided in three areas ruled from Damascus, then Beirut.

The obvious question is: How could the British government promise to Lord Rothschild the Ottomans' land? It could be viewed as an issue of timing. Great Britain was in the third year of World War I and gambled on the outcome of the war along the following lines: Turkey, which ruled the Ottoman Empire, decided to become an ally of Germany. The British needed allies of their own, so they made several promises (empty at the time). To the French, they promised that if they won the war, they would create two zones of influence over all the lands between the Mediterranean and the Persian Gulf, one British and the other one French. To the Jews, they gave the Balfour Declaration even though the Jews were not an official party in the war. With respect to the Arabs, they negotiated with the sharif of Mecca, Hussein ibn Ali, who was the great-grandfather of King Hussein of Jordan,[3] promising that he would have independence if he revolted against the Turks.

After World War I. The British won their gamble. Indeed, after the war, the League of Nations put Lebanon and Syria under French Mandate and Palestine and Transjordan under British Mandate (in 1922 Iraq was also placed under British Mandate). When those mandates took effect, the borders of Palestine changed again (1922–1926), when the French extended their influence on Syria and Lebanon.

The British kept their word to Hussein by rewarding his two sons,

2 Benny Morris, *One State, Two States: Resolving the Israel/Palestine Conflict* (New Haven: Yale University Press, 2009), 31.

3 King Hussein of Jordan, 1935–1999, ruled Jordan for forty-six years and was succeeded by his son Abdullah II, the current king.

Faisal and Abdullah. Faisal was pushed away from the throne of Syria by the French, so the British gave him the throne of Iraq. The other son of Hussein, Abdullah, was given Transjordan, which became the Hashemite Kingdom of Jordan (1949). Transjordan represented nearly four-fifths of Palestine, including all the land east of the Jordan River and the Dead Sea. At the same time, Britain issued a specific statement to exclude Transjordan from the provisions for a Jewish national home in the Palestine mandate, despite the fact that it was part of the biblical Land of Israel (which is described in biblical literature in varying terms but would seem to include at least some parts of the modern countries of Lebanon, Syria, Jordan, and Egypt). Britain also placed Fuad I over Egypt, which became a protectorate. That process of "king making" may seem odd. But the point of this background is that until today one wonders about the multitude of improbabilities that allowed the creation of the State of Israel and over which Jews had no control.

Another surprising but relevant aspect was the drawing of borders in relation to ethnicity. A rapid look at a map of Iraq reveals linear borders that bear little relation to the natural terrain. The British wanted to join two oil wells that were far away from each other (Kirkuk and Mosul), so they ended up combining three distinct groups: the Kurds, Sunnis, and Shiites. The logic in building this border was described as follows: "Churchill, well satisfied with his handiwork, frequently boasted that he created the Amirate of Transjordan by the stroke of his pen one bright Sunday afternoon and still had time to paint the magnificent views of Jerusalem before sundown."[4]

The last part of this "king making" has been summarized as follows: "Independence or autonomy for the Kurds, which had been on the

---

4   Avi Shlaim, *War and Peace in the Middle East: A Concise History* (New York: Penguin, 1994), 14.

agenda in 1921, somehow disappeared from the agenda in 1922, so there was to be no Kurdistan. In 1922, too, Britain imposed frontier agreements upon Ibn Saud that established boundaries between Saudi Arabia, Iraq and Kuwait."[5]

Now the British had to deliver on their promise to the Jews: the Supreme Council of the Allied Powers adopted the Balfour Declaration unanimously in April 1920, and in July 1922, in setting up the British Mandate over Palestine, the League of Nations incorporated the language of the Balfour Declaration.

This British heavy hand in reshaping the region may seem to have been partial to the Jews or to have favored them in some way. Here are the words of Churchill himself, who denies it in a speech in Parliament May 23, 1939:

> I cannot feel that we have accorded to the Arab race unfair treatment after the support which they gave us in the late War.... When I wrote this dispatch in 1922 I was advised by, among others, Colonel Lawrence, the truest champion of Arab rights whom modern times have known. He has recorded his opinion that the settlement was fair and just – his definite, settled opinion. Together we placed the Emir Abdulla in Transjordania, where he remains faithful and prosperous to this day....[6]

A summary shows the following succession of improbable events: (1) the first Zionist Congress makes a declaration in Basel that has nothing to back it up; (2) twenty years later, in the middle of World War I, the

---

5 David Fromkin, *A Peace to End All Peace: The Fall of the Ottoman Empire and the Creation of the Modern Middle East* (New York: Henry Holt and Company, 1989), 560.

6 Mordecai S. Chertoff, ed., *Zionism: A Basic Reader* (New York: Herzl Press, 1975), 47.

British make a declaration to Jews, who were not an official party to the war; (3) that declaration depends on the outcome of the war; (4) the gamble of the British succeeds and they reorganize the Middle East; (5) the League of Nations adopts the Balfour Declaration.

Initial Arab reaction. It is at that time that the Palestinian Arab national movement, supported by neighboring Arab countries, manifested itself by rejecting the Balfour Declaration and calling on the British to set up a government to be chosen by the Arabic-speaking people. The reason given for the rejection of the Balfour Declaration by the Third Palestine Arab Congress (1920) was because it was against "the laws of God and man" and because "Palestine is the holy land of the two Christian and Muslim worlds and…its destiny may not pass into other than Muslim and Christian hands."[7]

1922–1948: Emergence of the Jewish State

During the 1930s and 1940s, Jewish leaders (Chaim Weizmann, Abba Hillel Silver) were pleading their case in front of British and US audiences:

> Jews clung to Palestine all through Roman, Byzantine, Arab, Christian, and Turkish domination…. The effort to return to Palestine was unremitting through the ages. The living bond with Palestine was never broken. The hope to return became part of the Jews' creed. It echoed through the pages of his prayer book. His festivals were redolent of memories and hopes of Palestine. The Messianic hope which sustained the spirits of our people throughout the bleak centuries was essentially the hope of Israel's return to Palestine.[8]

During the same period, the mufti of Jerusalem, Haj Amin al-Husseini

---

7 Morris, *One State, Two States*, 88.

8 Chertoff, *Zionism*, 35.

(head of the Supreme Muslim Council in Palestine, chairman of the Arab Higher Committee), fomented revolts in Palestine. As soon as the Nazis came to power in 1933, he developed a collaboration with them to strengthen his hand in his fight against Jews in Palestine. After meeting Mussolini, Joachim von Ribbentrop (foreign minister), and Hitler himself, he set up shop in Berlin working with three agencies of the German government, spreading anti-Jewish broadcasts aimed at the Middle East.[9] A sample:

> One of the most prominent facets of the Jewish character is their exaggerated conceit and selfishness, rooted in their belief that they are the chosen people of God. There is no limit to their covetousness and they prevent others from enjoying the Good.... They have no pity and are known for their hatred, rivalry and hardness, as Allah has described them in the Koran.[10]

Palestinian leaders never recognized the historic connection of the Jews to the Land of Israel. This rejection continued all the way to the creation of the State of Israel, with a rhetoric that has been characterized as "starkly expulsionist."[11] On the morning following the Declaration of Independence, Israel was invaded from all sides.

Since the Founding: Arab Opposition to Israel

Fatah Leadership

The next official Palestinian position was that of the Palestinian National Covenant (1964), which declared: "The Balfour declaration [is] null and void" and "Zionism [is] an illegal movement and [the nations should]

---

9   Paul Berman, *The Flight of the Intellectuals* (Brooklyn: Melville House, 2010), 71.

10   Morris, *One State, Two States*, 105.

11   Ibid., 31.

outlaw its presence and activities."[12]

Then came the Fatah Constitution (1964) and the twenty-five years of Arafat's leadership. This is how Arafat's manipulative skills were described by Shimon Peres in 1993:

> It is not by pure luck that he has managed to survive for so long. Arafat began serving as head of the PLO during Lyndon Johnson's tenure as President of the United States, and managed to keep his job with the Nixon, Ford, Carter, Reagan, Bush, and Clinton administrations in power. With regard to Israel, he has stuck it out through Eshkol, Meir, Rabin, Begin, Shamir, Peres, Shamir again, and Rabin again. For a quarter of a century he has been leading a national coalition without nationhood, maintaining elections without being elected.[13]

When he appeared to negotiate with Israel under the sponsorship of Western countries, it was simply to gain the upper hand in his own power struggle with his internal enemies. For more details on Fatah-sponsored terrorism (including the first and second intifadas) and overtures for peace (Oslo Accords, Camp David), see the description provided in the previous chapter. The conclusion one draws from the relationship between Israel and the Fatah leadership was that the latter's opposition was not about the specific configuration of a Palestinian state but about the existence of Israel as a sovereign Jewish state.

Hamas Opposition and Control of Gaza

Arafat's deception was exposed by Hamas. Ironically, Western countries, particularly the United States, had put pressure on the Palestinian Arabs to become a "democracy," or at least to give some external signs that

---

12 Ibid., 110–11.

13 Peres, *The New Middle East*, 17.

they were on their way. Hamas's strategy utilized that pressure to its advantage and participated in "democratic" elections. Unlike Fatah, Hamas had been involved in "social and charitable" work among the Palestinian Arabs for some time and knew that they had won the hearts of their people. To the surprise of many, Hamas won the general elections in 2006 and took control of the Palestinian Legislative Council. In June 2007 they used their own methods and crushed – physically and militarily – all Fatah opposition. The survivors were expelled to the West Bank and Hamas inherited Gaza, which had been handed over by Israel when it decided to withdraw unilaterally in 2005.

Hamas's success drew on Arafat's tool, i.e., deception, but they based their position on religion. Hamas has two wings: one political, for "social and charitable work," and the other "military," meaning in charge of waging terrorist attacks in Israel. While Arafat and colleagues were accumulating in their Swiss bank accounts funds meant to build the Palestinian Arab economy, Hamas organizers were building schools, hospitals, and libraries to sway public opinion. They were busy recruiting young terrorists, and hiding their weapons and ammunitions among untouchable civilian sites such as hospitals. They spoke to Western journalists as if the political/social wing of Hamas was distinct from the military wing, so that the social wing could continue to receive external funding (supposedly to build the Palestinian Arab economy); on the other hand, their founder and leader Sheikh Ahmed Yassin was simultaneously speaking in Arabic of the two Hamas wings, saying: "We cannot separate the wings from the body. If we do so, the body will not be able to fly. Hamas is one body."[14]

Those who politicize hatred become so obsessed that they want it to transcend their lifetimes. Therefore, they teach it in textbooks to children

14 Bard, *Myths and Facts*, 267.

used as *shahids* (martyrs – dying for Allah is the greatest glory). We know that "children who grow up in such an environment tend to absorb the hatred around them and the sense of a need for vengeance as effortlessly as the air they breathe, thus perpetuating them for another generation."[15] In the end, Hamas won because they were able to deceive the West, Fatah itself, and a large segment of the Palestinian Arab people.

The Fatah-to-Hamas switch in Gaza was important because it revealed the religion-based causes of the Palestinian opposition, as written in their Covenant of the Islamic Resistance Movement: "The Movement's program is Islam.... Nationalism...is part of the religious creed." Hamas "strives to raise the banner of Allah over every inch of Palestine."[16] According to Paul Berman, Hamas drew its ideology from the well of the Muslim Brotherhood and quotes in its charter the Brotherhood leader Hassan al-Banna: "Israel will be established and will stay established until Islam nullifies it, as it nullified what was before it..."[17] In agreement with that assessment, the historian Benny Morris summarized Hamas's position: "Hence, the destruction of the Jewish state is Allah's command."[18]

There is a perception that Hamas's originality was its focus on an Islam-based conflict with Israel; however, as early as forty years before, the Palestinian National Covenant's position was also based on Islam (1964): Palestinian Arabs should "move forward on the path of a holy war [jihad] until complete and final victory.... Judaism, because it is a divine religion, is not a nationality with independent existence."[19] Similarly, the

---

15 Dozier, *Why We Hate*, 247.

16 Morris, *One State, Two States*, 155–57.

17 Berman, *The Flight of the Intellectuals*, 39.

18 Morris, *One State, Two States*, 158.

19 Ibid., 110–11.

Declaration of Independence of the PLO (1988) ended with: "Say: O God, Master of the Kingdom, Thou givest the Kingdom to whom Thou wilt, and seizes the Kingdom from whom Thou wilt, Thou exalted whom Thou wilt, and Thou abasest whom Thou wilt; in Thy hand is the good; Thou art powerful over everything."[20]

If Fatah's opposition to Israel also had a "religious" basis, what was the difference between Fatah and Hamas? None, according to the Anglo-Palestinian historian Yezid Sayigh, cited by Morris: Fatah's "ultimate goal" from its inception "was…to destroy…Israel as an economic, political, and military entity and restore Palestine as it still existed in the minds of most Palestinians, the [Arab] homeland that was before 1948…. There was little difference between Fatah and any other Palestinian group in this respect…. There was little room for the Jews in this outlook."[21]

If so, how can we explain the 2007 killing of Fatah supporters by Hamas in Gaza? Fatah was crushed because they pretended to recognize the existence of a Jewish state. According to Hamas's radical Islamist version of Islam, that is a crime punishable by death.

Since its onset, the opposition of Palestinian Arabs to Israel was not just based on a land title dispute. Such a disagreement could have been resolved in an international court, and indeed it was adjudicated by the United Nations vote in 1947. With the Fatah to Hamas switch, it became apparent that for a century, Palestinian Arabs of all shades had consistently based their opposition to Israel on the fact that it is a Jewish state. That hostility rested on some selective interpretation of their own religion, Islam.

---

20   Ibid., 125–26.

21   Ibid., 115.

Shiite Hatred: It's Not about Land

It is important to distinguish between Arab concerns about land and Arab religious concerns. The former is what has been expressed to Western countries while the latter is for internal consumption. This distinction explains two critical developments: the birth of Hezbollah and the role of Iran.

After the success of the Iranian Revolution, Khomeini had been looking for an opportunity to expand his revolution to other Shia population centers in the Middle East. His success in Iraq was limited because the Shias felt strongly about their Iraqi identity and he would have to contend with Saddam Hussein. So he targeted Lebanon for several reasons: (1) more than 40 percent of the Lebanese population is Shia, (2) Lebanon was easy to destabilize since it was already divided between Christians and Muslims, (3) Khomeini's revolution had no interest in Christian or Sunni Arabs. His opportunity arose in 1982 when Israel remained in the south of Lebanon (First Lebanon War). To have ownership of his own force, he weakened the local Shia movement (Amal) and built his own Shia group by the name of Hezbollah (from a split-off faction of Amal).

As Iranian-American scholar Vali Nasr explained it in his analysis of the trajectory of the Shiite movement, "Iran's ties to Hezbollah run deep. It was Iranian clerics and Revolutionary Guards commanders who first organized Hezbollah in the 1980s, and since then Teheran has bankrolled and armed Hezbollah's war machine."[22] Hezbollah fostered the cult of martyrdom within Islam to a new level: "Martyrdom gave suicide bombing a gloss of Islamic religious legitimacy."[23] That approach turned

---

22 Vali Nasr, *The Shia Revival: How Conflicts within Islam Will Shape the Future* (New York: W.W. Norton, 2006), 269.

23 Ibid., 142.

out to be successful. From the outset, Hezbollah was dedicated to jihad against Israel even though there was no land dispute per se between Hezbollah and Israel. It was pure Islamist-based hatred.

Hezbollah planned for quite some time: they built their forces and positions and fabricated a war in the summer of 2006 by kidnapping Israeli soldiers from within Israel. In addition, they fired rockets on the north of Israel. Israel retaliated but in spite of the strength of the IDF, Hezbollah was not defeated because they were prepared and their forces were concealed among civilians. Hezbollah, just like Hamas, used civilians as shields, knowing that the availability of instantaneous worldwide visual media coverage would paralyze the Israelis. After thirty-four days and the loss of hundreds of Israeli soldiers and civilians, Israel agreed to a cease-fire and pulled out of Lebanon.

Hezbollah became heroes on the Arab street. In addition, since they were the local arm of Iran, this victory propelled the Iranian regime politically in the region. Hezbollah concluded an alliance with Syria, which always wanted to maintain its influence in Lebanon. At that point, the Shia revival was achieved: the Iran-Hezbollah axis had three connected points and constituted "a Shia front cutting through the heart of the Arab world. It connected the two most radical parts of the Shia world, Iran and Lebanon, as something like the two wings of Khomeini's project."[24]

An interesting question arises: Since there is a chronic ruthless war between Shiites and Sunnis in Iraq and elsewhere in the Muslim world, why is it that both branches of Islam are united in their commitment to war with Israel? Because the "true" brand of Islam will be the one that will rid the Middle East of Israel. Therefore, Israel became a "pawn" in an intra-Islamic battle.

---

24 Ibid., 143.

Islam versus Islamists

To understand the motivations of Hamas and Hezbollah, an important distinction should be made between Islam and Islamists. According to authors who have studied the Islamist movement, Islamists are modern Muslim leaders who utilize Islam to promote a violent political agenda. The birth of the Islamist movement is dated to the formation of the Muslim Brotherhood in 1928 by Hassan al-Banna, in Egypt. Some characteristics of this movement are of interest: "The Brotherhood became a political force.... It was also a religious movement, pious and observant. It was intellectually vigorous. It was educationally active. The Brotherhood was athletics oriented... and welfare oriented. The Brotherhood was also paramilitary, if only covertly, with an exterior appearance of law-respecting cautiousness."[25]

The "Supreme Guide" of the movement, Hassan al-Banna, taught patience and willingness to endure harsh suffering, particularly death. He wrote: "Degradation and dishonor are the results of the love of this world and the fear of death. Therefore prepare for jihad and be lovers of death."[26] This movement grew rapidly and spread from Egypt to other Arab and Muslim countries. Of particular relevance is the Palestinian branch led by the grand mufti of Jerusalem, Haj Amin al-Husseini. Research based on recent archives demonstrates a close association between leaders of the Islamist movement and Nazi leaders. There was a close collaboration in Berlin between the mufti of Jerusalem and Hitler as described above. Also relevant is the spread of Muslim Brotherhood ideas to the Shiite branch of Islam, as elaborated by Ayatollah Khomeini. With this background, the ideology and growth of Hamas, al-Qaeda, and Hezbollah become understandable. For example, the spiritual and

---

25 Berman, *The Flight of the Intellectuals*, 31–32.

26 Ibid., 33.

political leader of Hamas was Sheikh Ahmed Yassin, who was the leader of the Palestine branch of the Muslim Brotherhood.

Israel's Creation Validates Judaism

Islamists interpret the creation of the State of Israel as the realization of basic claims of Judaism, and this ends up validating Judaism as a religion. Therefore, they believe that they cannot stand back and let this happen unchallenged.

Through their Islamist political lenses, they interpret Islam and Judaism as mutually exclusive.[27] If history appears to assist Jews by allowing them to build a state, it is automatically a discredit to Islam. Reestablishment of ancient Israel on its land must be reversed at all cost, even to the point of martyrdom.

First, there is the discomfort or shame associated with the fact that the State of Israel was built under everyone's watch, and through a succession of events that were completely improbable. How could a few thousand Jews who escaped pogroms and concentration camps be capable of fabricating a state from swampy and desert lands? Early Zionists came as a trickle of individuals, many of whom left their countries illegally and were stopped by the British blockade. To begin with, there were never enough Jews to create a state. To achieve the increase in population from 85,000 in 1914 to 630,000 in 1948, European Jewry had paid the price of the Holocaust.

At the time of the UN vote on the partition resolution in 1947, Jerusalem was excluded from the partition plan. In the months that followed the UN vote, Arabs waged a merciless war against Jews in a territory without borders. The British Mandate was ending, and Britain was about to pull out. In view of the violence, the UN considered revoking the 1947

27 Koran, Sura 2:125, 127.

partition plan and putting all of Palestine under UN governance. To avoid such an outcome, the National Council, Jewish settlement members, and heads of the Zionist movement walked to Tel Aviv Independence Hall on Friday, May 14, 1948 (5 Iyar) at 5 p.m. and signed the Declaration of Independence.

This was immediately followed by the attack of five armies.[28] The outcome of that war was highly implausible, going in favor of the Israelis, resulting in an increase in territory at the Armistice of 1949. Although the Balfour Declaration had been made in 1917, the events that led to Israeli independence essentially unfurled from the 1947 UN Partition Plan, resulting in the establishment within one year of an independent Jewish state on a piece of land that had been under Muslim control for four centuries. There was no historical precedent for such a succession of events, all improbable yet all coming true.

Another difficult aspect of the succession of events that led to the creation of the State of Israel was that they appeared to agree with claims made by some religious Jews in Israel who viewed them as "miraculous." Those claims included notions such as: (1) the Jewish people were uniquely capable of remaining one distinct people; (2) when the Jewish people were not on "their" land, no nation was allowed to establish itself on it permanently. This last point is particularly troublesome because it corresponds to the unanswered question addressed at the beginning of this chapter: What prevented the Palestinian Arab population from coalescing into one nation and forming a state like Egypt or Turkey before or during the four centuries of Ottoman rule? Both religious Jews and Islamists believe that the real implication was not what but Who prevented it.

Based on the above, it becomes understandable why Iranian president

---

28   Egypt, Syria, Transjordan, Lebanon, and Iraq.

Ahmadinejad would convene a conference called "The World without Zionism" in 2005, and proclaim the imperative of extermination of the State of Israel even as he faced issues of trust vis-à-vis Western governments regarding Iranian development of nuclear weapons. It also becomes understandable why that same person would publicly participate in Holocaust denial.

Conclusions

The objective of this analysis was to learn why or how Israelis comprehend the opposition of Fatah, Hamas, and Hezbollah in ways that created internal fault lines.

We asked: How are we to understand their feelings toward Israel? In spite of the profound differences that exist between Hamas and Fatah on one hand, and between Shiites and Sunnis on the other, they share the determination to obliterate Israel. The issue is not just a Palestinian Arab state or its boundaries. Tragically, during the decades of strife, the needs of the Palestinian Arab people were not truly addressed. When Hamas focused on its own people, it was only to use civilians as a shield to fight a war with effective publicity. If the issues were of a classically political nature, there would be hope for a resolution; indeed there is ample historical precedent for deep hatred between sworn enemies that was eventually overcome (France and Germany, for example, or Catholics and Protestants in Northern Ireland).

This analysis suggests that the hatred of Fatah, Hamas, and Hezbollah is rooted in an interpretation of Islam by modern Islamists that makes it mutually exclusive with the existence of the State of Israel. As Rush Dozier explains, "Those who hate tend to obsess about past injuries as well as current and future threats they perceive.... Because of this obsessive thinking, there is a tendency to feel trapped in a zero-sum

game that can be escaped only by the destruction of one's adversary."[29]
Hatred, in a perverse way, provides a sense of victimization, a high
moral ground, and an avoidance of self-evaluation.

If that analysis is correct, then the principle issue faced by Israel is that
it is trapped at the epicenter of an intra-Islamic problem. Islam is torn by
the profound Shia-Sunni conflict and by political Islamists who appear
to have the upper hand. Israel just happens to be caught in the middle.
A consequence is that Israelis have no reason to transform all that
external hatred into internal divisions. Such divisions turn into discord
and disunity that are baseless since the main issues are in fact intra-
Islamic. Israelis face a situation requiring that they protect themselves
against the cult of martyrdom until someone with enough authority in the
Islamic world arises and uncouples Israel from the Islamists' politically
motivated interpretations of Islam. Alternatively, Israelis may have to
wait for enough Palestinian Arabs and Muslim citizens to ask why both
religions cannot coexist even with different beliefs – or simply, why
both religions cannot be valid for different people, letting history take
its course.

---

29 Dozier, *Why We Hate*, 260.

7

Western Hostility:
The New Antisemitism

As shown in the last chapter, the opposition of Islamists to the State of Israel is a century-old phenomenon that is based in religious issues. Every generation of Israelis has had to deal with it, either during military service or reserve duty or in everyday life during the period of the two intifadas. Political and media attacks on Israel emanating from the Western world constitute a more recent behavior, distinct from the United Nations condemnations of the past decades that were fomented by the large number of Muslim countries and their allies.

This Western hostility is a new phenomenon, only a decade old. It originated in Europe and seemed to involve all of the world's democracies (except perhaps for the United States). It was manifested as open, blatant hostility that justified itself by condemning the behavior of the Israeli government toward Palestinian Arabs. Most troubling were the tensions it generated within Israeli society, because this external opposition was condoned or even fueled by certain post-Zionist segments within Israel (primarily writers and academics). Other Israelis wondered whether it was a rebirth of the centuries-old antisemitism. If so, it contradicted one of Herzl's basic premises: antisemitism would end when the Jews would have their own state. Furthermore, if Western hostility is linked to the Palestinian issue, which is a century old, why did this anti-Israel movement manifest itself when the State of Israel was sixty years old?

Westerners in an Islamist World

Facts

Due diligence requires that we ascertain that this new European opposition is not just the result of Jewish hypersensitivity. Manifestations of this opposition came from a variety of sources, obviously unrelated. Objective expressions could be quantified by the absolute number of antisemitic incidents such as attacks on Jews and synagogues as well as cemetery desecrations. Anti-Israel bias was also apparent in media articles, editorials, commentaries, Internet blogs, rallies, and demonstrations in major cities. Additionally, it was particularly visible on university campuses. These types of manifestations were documented in France, England, Germany, Belgium, Greece, Spain, and Italy.

The most obvious example was England, where the new antisemitic tone of the public discourse involved major outlets such as the British Broadcasting Corporation (BBC), political leaders at the highest echelons such as Members of Parliament, and even the wife of the prime minister. Some British actions included boycotts of Israelis and Israeli products. For example, Britain's Association of University Teachers initiated boycotts of Israeli academics (2005). Also, Britain's National Association of Teachers in Further and Higher Education accused Israel of "apartheid policies" and, as a consequence, pushed for a boycott of Israeli academics (2006).

Another example is the Norwegian intellectual Jostein Gaarder (author of *Sophie's World*), who stated in 2006: "We no longer recognize the State of Israel.... The State of Israel, in its current form, is history."[1] In some countries such as Spain and Greece, the anti-Jewish attitudes did not make sense since Jews represent less than 1 percent of the population. Another proof that this assessment was not Jewish hypersensitivity came from objective voices like that of Oriana Fallaci, an Italian journalist who fought with the partisans during World War II: "I find it shameful that in France – the France of 'Liberty, Equality and Fraternity' – synagogues are torched, Jews are terrorized, and their cemeteries profaned... that in Holland and Germany and Denmark youngsters show off the kaffiyeh like the vanguard of Mussolini displayed the stick and Fascist emblem... that in almost every European university, Palestinian students take over and nurture anti-Semitism."[2]

Rationales

This new European-based anti-Israel attitude was perplexing because of its breadth and spontaneity. Clearly it must have had multiple origins. Some proposed rationales were within the realm of traditional politics. Some countries could oppose the policies of the government of the State of Israel for a variety of self-serving reasons – for example, concern about the attitudes of twenty million Muslims who now live in different European countries. Also, some Europeans resent what seems like a

---

1   Jostein Gaarder, "God's Chosen People," *Aftenposten*, August 5, 2006.

2   Oriana Fallaci, "Sull'antisemitismo" [On antisemitism], *Panorama*, April 18, 2002, translated from the original Italian by David A. Harris, *in In the Trenches: Selected Speeches and Writings of an American Jewish Activist*, vol. 3, 2002 2003 (Jersey City, NJ: Ktav, 2004), 361.

systematic American support for Israel based on the belief that the Jewish lobby has an "iron grip" on American foreign policy.

Other rationales were linked to increased election successes of right-wing parties in several countries or traditional religious roots (remnants of anti-Jewish stereotypes such as those propagated by the Greek Orthodox Church, the Anglican Church, or even British Catholic publications). Some were more difficult to qualify but still troubling for Israel, such as European newspapers (Britain's *Guardian*, France's *Le Monde*) calling for the UN to establish an inquiry regarding a purported "massacre" committed by Israeli soldiers in Jenin (2002). Others were reminders of prior events such as the attempts to have the UN World Conference against Racism in Durban, South Africa, adopt language repeating the accusation that Zionism is equivalent to racism. But the principal question was: What is the rationale for holding Israel responsible for the welfare of Palestinian Arabs when their own leaders and other states in the region or in Europe are not earnest in their own efforts?

The classic answer is that Israel is no longer threatened or powerless but appears as a warmongering colonial power. It is now viewed as having displaced people who became refugees because their land was usurped in 1948. Each new act of construction in one of the Israeli "settlements" is perceived by the Islamists and their Western backers as a repeat of this original "offense." Furthermore, settlers are often motivated by the fulfillment of messianic beliefs, delegitimizing them in the eyes of Europeans who consider these beliefs invalid and certainly not a basis for land ownership.

Another rationale discussed below is that many Europeans still feel guilty about the Holocaust, and criticism of Israel helps them address repressed guilt. They purge their dark past when they can sit in judgment of Israel and Zionists all over the world. Support of Israel is unwarranted on moral grounds because Israel has racial laws and displays criminal behavior (see the explanation of Alain Finkielkraut below). An aspect that is relevant to Europeans is the relationship between the creation of the State of Israel and the outcomes of World War I and World War II (as described at the beginning of chapter 6). For those reasons, some European governments and leaders are impatient to achieve a solution to the "Palestinian problem" and are also irritated by Israel's insistence on its own conditions for the resolution.

Palestinian-Western Link

What is the link between Palestinian Arabs and Europeans? Two sets of analyses are presented. The first set is from non-Israeli authors including two French philosophers (Bernard-Henri Lévy and Alain Finkielkraut) and two American writers (Paul Berman and Shelby Steele). The second set is from Israeli authors, including the former government minister Natan Sharansky and the two writers Caroline Glick and Daniel Gordis.

Hypocrisy

The following piece by Bernard-Henri Lévy was written in response to the disingenuous and one-sided world reaction to Israel's self-defense in the May 2010 Gaza flotilla incident, in which six Turkish ships violated naval blockades on Gaza. Five of the ships were taken into custody by the Israeli military without incident, but the *Mavi Marmara*, carrying armed Islamic terrorists, ambushed Israeli soldiers with lethal results. In his unique and eloquent style, Levy addresses the collusion between Palestinian Arabs and the rest of the world and the resulting hypocrisy.

Disinformation: The utter silence, throughout the world, about Hamas' incredible attitude now that the flotilla has carried out its symbolic duty, which was to catch the Jewish State out and relaunch, as never before, the process of demonization....

...Gaza's children having been nothing more than a human shield for the Islamist gang who took power by force three years ago, or cannon fodder or media vignettes, their games or their wishes are the last thing anyone worries about there, but who says so?

Who shows the slightest indignation? *Libération* recently ran an awful headline, "Israel, Pirate State," which if words still mean anything, can only contribute to the delegitimization of the Hebrew State.

Who will dare to explain that, if there is a hostage taker, one who coldly and unscrupulously takes advantage of people's suffering and, in particular, that of the children – in sum, a pirate – in Gaza, it is not Israel but Hamas?[3]

Bernard-Henri Lévy's words require no additional elucidation.

Palestinian Arabs as "Victims of Holocaust Victims"

Alain Finkielkraut's analysis,[4] written in 2005, attempts to explain how Palestine has become a "Universal Cause" by posing the following questions: "To what does Palestine owe this extraordinary privilege? What is the source of this unequaled, unprecedented fixation? Why has the keffiyeh become a universal symbol of rebellion? And finally, why the Palestinians, and not the Chechens, the Tibetans, the Bosnians, the Tutsis, or the Sudanese?"

His analysis points to the link made by today's humanists between Jews as Holocaust victims and Israelis as supposed murderers, who mutilate and assassinate Palestinian Arab children. These European humanists

---

3   Bernard-Henri Lévy, "Why I Defend Israel," *The Huffington Post*, June 7, 2010.

4   Alain Finkielkraut, "The Religion of Humanity and the Sin of the Jews," *Azure* 21 (2005): 23.

define "state Zionism as that which converts the 'capital of victimhood' into the 'capital of power and violence.'"[5] Finkielkraut points out the opportunity for exculpation presented by condemnation of Israel, for "if those toward whom we behaved shamefully are now behaving shamefully themselves, then there is no more need to feel ashamed.... In short, the Palestinian cause has provided a humanity weary of apologizing for having abandoned six million Jews to their deaths an unhoped-for opportunity to relieve itself of the burden of repentance."[6]

For these European humanists, the Palestinian Arabs have become "the victims of the victims." These humanists are not antisemitic because they forgot the Holocaust, but precisely "on account of the reversal of memory," in Finkielkraut's phrase. They accuse Israel and the Jews, because they, the humanists, remember. Thus they feel free to denounce the Jews not as Jewish traitors but as "traitors to their Jewishness"; therefore, their slogan of hate became "Down with the Jews, no longer Jewish at all!"[7]

These humanists-leftists and their Palestinian Arab allies use the Holocaust as a basis for an attack on the foundational identity of the State of Israel. In the context of the Holocaust, "the definition of Israel as a Jewish state is precisely what undermines Israel's legitimacy in the eyes of much of the world."[8] The very fact of a state aligning itself with an identity must mean that within it any other identity is squelched and trampled upon; declaring itself to be a Jewish state perforce makes Israel an apartheid state. Based on this logic, the State of Israel's Jewishness is an offense to the memory of the Holocaust and to the leftists' universal vision of the world. Therefore, the only way to repair this offense is to

---

5   Ibid.

6   Ibid.

7   Ibid.

8   Ibid.

transform Israel into a multi- or postnational state.

This insightful analysis by Alain Finkielkraut should be used as part of the take-home message delivered to young Jews who visit Holocaust memorials and museums of tolerance. In Israel, Palestinian Arab enemies of the State of Israel do visit the Yad Vashem Holocaust Museum and produce their own take-home message, saying essentially: "We are the victims of these Holocaust victims." This defilement of the memory of the Holocaust should be addressed because it is even more insidious than the old Holocaust denial campaigns.

Islamists in the Western World

Paul Berman provides another dimension of the Palestinian-Western link, focusing on the coverage of Islamist doctrines and ideas by Western intellectuals, thinkers, and journalists. In his recent book *The Flight of the Intellectuals*,[9] he researched the history of the Islamist movement and brought into the open the cowardice of American intellectuals. He exposed their inability to comprehend and their unwillingness to report on the thinking of Islamists. Because he addressed a sensitive issue and took on the establishment, his book was highly criticized. This is how he responded to the criticism in an editorial piece entitled "What You Can't Say about Islamism" in the *Wall Street Journal* (July 10, 2010):

> In our present Age of the Zipped Lip, you are supposed to avoid making any of the following inconvenient observations about the history and doctrines of the Islamist movement:
>
> You are not supposed to observe that Islamism is a modern, instead of an ancient, political tendency, which arose in a spirit of fraternal harmony with the fascists of Europe in the 1930s and '40s.
>
> You are not supposed to point out that Nazi inspirations have

9 Paul Berman, *The Flight of the Intellectuals* (New York: Melville House Publishing, 2010).

visibly taken root among present-day Islamists, notably in regard to the demonic nature of Jewish conspiracies and the virtues of genocide.

And you are not supposed to mention that, by inducing a variety of journalists and intellectuals to maintain a discreet and respectful silence on these awkward matters, the Islamist preachers and ideologues have succeeded in imposing on the rest of us their own categories of analysis....

Two Explanations of Hatred

In another analysis of the Gaza flotilla incident, Shelby Steele proposes the following hypothesis to explain why "world opinion" does not miss an opportunity to scapegoat the Jews and the State of Israel:[10]

1. The Western world suffers from a "deficit of moral authority": Israel is seen as a white colonial state while Palestinian Arabs are occupied, impoverished victims; the Western world knows that this is not correct but cannot afford to contradict that view for fear of appearing imperialist, supremacist, and xenophobic.

2. "Palestinians and much of the Middle East are driven to militancy and war not by legitimate complaints against Israel or the West but by an internalized sense of inferiority"; even if the Palestinian Arabs were to fulfill their wish list and become able to build a new militarized state, "they would wake up the next morning still hounded by a sense of inferiority."[11]

3. The "quickest cover for inferiority is hatred"; hatred provides Palestinians with "the innocence that defines victims," with "moral

---

10 Shelby Steele, "Israel and the Surrender of the West," *Wall Street Journal*, June 21, 2010. Shelby Steele is a senior fellow at Stanford University's Hoover Institution and also a member of the Working Group on Islamism and the International Order.

11 Ibid.

superiority." Most of the Muslim world shares this "attraction to the consolations of hatred."[12]

Herzl's Failed Prophecy

The former Israeli minister Natan Sharansky wrote two insightful analyses delving into the "new versus old" antisemitism found in Western countries. In the first (written in 2003),[13] he wrote as a person who had experienced antisemitism firsthand in the Soviet Union and compared it to this "new" European version. He concluded that they are different because what he had known was government sponsored while the more recent type was (at least officially) opposed by the governments. But one new dimension is that the illusion that democracy would be "an infallible antidote to active hatred of Jews" is forever shattered.

In the second analysis,[14] he courageously addressed Herzl's "failed prophecy" that antisemitism would end through a national solution – that is, when the Jews would have a home. According to Herzl, with a state, the Jews would achieve "recognition as a nation" and "the individual Jew would finally be able to live in peace." Sharansky points out that unfortunately, "over the half century since the Jewish state was founded, it has consistently been a lightning rod of hatred and enmity," hatred from the Arab world and much broader-based hatred: "The old antisemitism takes the form of anti-Zionism. As far as the world is concerned, the Jews are Israel, and Israel the Jews." He concludes by posing and answering the following questions: "Why was Herzl's vision not realized? How is it that the Jewish state was established but anti-Semitism still exists? The problem, perhaps, lay with Herzl's failure to divine the true nature

---

12 Ibid.

13 Natan Sharansky, "On Hating the Jews," *Commentary* 116 (November 2003): 26–34.

14 Sharansky, "The Political Legacy of Theodor Herzl," 87.

of anti-Semitism – a hatred that, throughout history, has always been directed at the very core of Jewish identity."[15]

Sharansky divides the history of antisemitism into three phases, corresponding to the world's perception of the core of Jewish identity: first, antisemitism was directed against the Jews' monotheistic religion, then against the sense of belonging to one people and tradition, and finally the State of Israel, as the perceived core of Jewish identity, became the focus of antisemitism.

Europe versus United States

In 2003, Caroline Glick posed these questions: "[What has Israel done] to cause this rash of Jew hatred? Is our army's treatment of the Palestinians responsible? Are the Israelis who live in Judea, Samaria and Gaza to blame for Europe's steadily rising comfort level with public expressions of anti-Semitism?"[16]

She answers by suggesting that the reason for the shift in support by European countries has to do with the new Europe-United States competition for world influence and projection of power. Europe thinks that the United States can no longer function alone, ignoring what others feel or think. Europe also thinks that it has become indispensable to the United States; the United States may have power but Europe has a cultural superiority. Therefore, the United States should join European governments in their view that Israel's right to sovereignty should be conditional upon the acceptance by Israel's enemies of its right to exist. Thus, according to her analysis, "There is a direct connection between Europe's anti-Semitism and its anti-Americanism."[17]

15 Ibid.

16 Glick, *Shackled Warrior*, 323.

17 Ibid., 326.

Impact on Israel

In his analysis, Daniel Gordis makes two key points:

1. These global attacks on Israel are not just uncomfortable or unpleasant for Israelis and other Jews, they are extremely dangerous. The Holocaust showed that the writings of antisemitic intellectuals and academics created a framework of dehumanization that allowed the genocide to take place. Here too, the campaign to delegitimize the State of Israel is waged at multiple levels: denying its right to security, then accusing Israel of war crimes, and finally uprooting the state by destroying the historical links between the people and the land.[18] The result of these concerted attacks is "the gradual and subtle preparation of the world for the idea of a world without Israel."[19]

2. Even worse than the above assessment is his description of the state of mind of the Israeli government and population. "Many Israelis are not up for a persistent and long-term battle against international public opinion.... Unable to articulate thoughtful responses to these varied accusations and calls for Israel's end, some have joined forces with those calls, wondering aloud whether, in fact, the Jewish state still makes sense, and whether it is still worth fighting for.... Israelis have tired of fighting and of sending their children to war, but they have no idea how to settle the conflicts that consume them."[20]

Gordis sounds an alarm call to world Jewry to get involved and participate in devising an appropriate course of action to overcome these challenges.

---

18 Dore Gold, "The Challenge to Israel's Legitimacy," in *Israel at 60* (Jerusalem Center for Public Affairs, 2009), 3.

19 Gordis, *Saving Israel*, 82.

20 Ibid., 216.

Conclusions

This analysis of non-Muslim hatred facing Israel shows that the umbrella effect of the Holocaust in the Western world had run its course. Humanist movements who criticize Israel did not forget the Holocaust; on the contrary, they use it against Israel. As Natan Sharansky sees it, given the hatred leveled at the State of Israel, "That state – the world's Jew – has the distinction of challenging two separate political/moral orders simultaneously: the order of the Arab and Muslim Middle East, and the order that prevails in Western Europe."[21] These two orders target not the State of Israel but Israel's identity, its core Jewishness, its legality, and its legitimacy.

How should Israeli and Diaspora Jews react to global hatred?

Israel cannot wait until its enemies in the Middle East or the Western world realize that, as long as they behave as prisoners of pathological hatred toward Israel, they end up hurting the Palestinian Arabs. Clearly, there should be a debate within Israeli society about the optimum behavior toward Palestinian Arabs, especially because they have been used by their own leaders and other states as pawns and were never provided basic necessities: a life with independence and dignity.

At the same time, if Israelis understand the underlying basis of this global hatred, they will avoid turning it into a divisive wedge within Israeli society. They should not allow external criticism to turn into self-doubt, inner malaise, and insecurity about the future. One constructive response to this external hatred would be to focus on their own internal hatred. Jonathan Sacks, the chief rabbi of Great Britain, advocates this approach as he implores, "May we protest against gentile antisemitism without practising Jewish philosemitism, *ahavat yisrael*? May we ask the nations of the world to live at peace with Jews without first learning to live at peace with one another?"[22]

A specific proposal to this effect is made in the next chapter.

---

21   Sharansky, "On Hating the Jews," 26–34.

22   Sacks, *One People*, 227.

Part 3

Solutions for Hatred

8

Reaction to Global Hatred: *Arevut* Proposal

In the last decade, the State of Israel found itself at the center of a worldwide antisemitic storm and became the main source of antisemitism for Diaspora Jews. It became apparent that the whole world "increasingly hates Jews because it increasingly hates Israel."[1] Several Israeli writers have described Israel's reaction to this isolation; it was not the typical self-assured and resilient attitude that Israel had exhibited in the past. Israelis, particularly the younger generation, were caught off guard by this new broad-based hatred to the point that basic issues emerged about Israel's identity, its purpose, and survival: "Israelis themselves are no longer certain whether the battle for their existence is worth its costs."[2] These issues are of concern not just for Israelis but for all Diaspora

---

1 Sharansky, "On Hating the Jews," 26–34.

2 Gordis, *Saving Israel*, 82.

Jews. In this chapter, we take the position that this self-examination is a positive step because it shows that solutions cannot come from focusing on one's enemies, but rather must come from within. An approach to curb baseless hatred and build *arevut* is proposed.

Spectrum of Solutions from Israeli Authors

Let us begin with constructive solutions proposed by a spectrum of Israeli authors who have examined and written on these issues.

Daniel Gordis

In his book entitled *Saving Israel*, Daniel Gordis proposed that solutions can be found in focusing on repairing the deficiencies that led to the current crisis of self-doubt. He suggested that the original "disdain for Jewish tradition" of the founding secular Zionists produced "utter Jewish ignorance" in the later generations and that "passion for Jewish sovereignty can subside when Jewish literacy is a vestige of the past." Gordis suggests that Judaism should be restored "to the heart of Israel's national debate," even though it will not be easy since many Israelis have inherited an "antipathy to religious ritual." In Gordis's view, Judaism is no longer merely a matter of personal preference because Jewishness is a matter of national security.

Aaron Ciechanover

A similar message was recently proposed by Aaron Ciechanover, winner of the 2004 Nobel Prize in Chemistry:

> I deeply regret that I cannot see anyone in the ranks of today's leadership who acts out of a true concern for the promotion of the country's spiritual affairs, and whose past and present actions serve as an example and a model to be imitated and esteemed. I cannot identify a single leader who could inspire the multitudes to social,

educational, and cultural activism.... The era of Israel's founder, David Ben-Gurion – who, in even darker days for our country, started a Jewish Bible study group in his own home, and authored the book *Ben-Gurion Looks at the Bible* – ended all too soon, and certainly before it managed to put down strong roots.[3]

Therefore, he proposes an "investment of effort and resources in the study of the tradition, history, and archaeology of the Jewish people in Israel and the diaspora."[4] His objective is to heal the fatal disease called "the depletion of spirit." Interestingly, another Israeli Nobel Prize winner, Professor Yisrael Aumann (quoted by Daniel Gordis[5]), makes a similar suggestion that any solution to the threats that Israel faces must come "from within us."

Caroline Glick

In her columns collected in the recent book *Shackled Warrior*, Caroline Glick stated: "Today, the Jewish people, in Israel and throughout the world, find ourselves under attack from all quarters. The rise of anti-Semitism globally, and particularly in the Islamic world, finds us in a period of grave self-doubt. Like the Europeans, our ability to defend ourselves against the swelling ranks of haters is dependent on our ability as a people and as individuals to embrace our identity as Jews."[6] She also asserted: "Today we understand that being a light unto the nations means setting an example of loyalty to our traditions of valor and simple human decency, with the hope that others will follow, and not attempting to appease murderers and begging for acceptance."[7]

---

3 Aaron Ciechanover, letter to the editor, *Azure* 31 (2008).

4 Ibid.

5 Gordis, *Saving Israel*, 112.

6 Glick, *Shackled Warrior,* 423.

7 Ibid., 411.

In the first quote, Glick proposes that we return to and celebrate our identity as Jews, but she is not specific about the role of religion, per se. In the second quote, she brings up the mission of Israel as "a light unto the nations," which is quite bold. Furthermore, she characterizes the path to the achievement of this goal as loyalty to our traditions of valor and human decency. By what mechanism these objectives could be achieved on a national scale is not described.

Natan Sharansky

In an article entitled "The Political Legacy of Theodor Herzl," written in 2005,[8] Natan Sharansky offered the following description of the state of various communities in Israel:

> Without Jewish history, and without Jewish culture, it is impossible to make a mosaic. What is being produced in Israel instead is a society made up of distinct groups that tend to keep mostly to themselves, put sectarian interests above national ones, and compete for control of the country. For a society that is still very much in its formative period, and in many ways still fighting for its survival, this does not bode well. This trend is all the more dangerous because the cultural vacuum is increasingly being filled by a post-Zionist vision of society, in which religious and secular, Ashkenazim and Sephardim, Jews and Arabs will all live side by side – but with nothing to bind them together.

This author points out the consequences of trying to produce in Israel a new type of secular "Sabra" Jew. Like the previous authors, he proposes a return to traditional Jewish values, though the method of doing so is not clear.

---

8 Sharansky, "The Political Legacy of Theodor Herzl," 96.

Rabbi Ian Pear

In his recent (2008) book entitled *The Accidental Zionist*, Rabbi Ian Pear proposes to build a Diaspora-Israel bridge. Emotional and intellectual approaches are used to show how the message of "ethical monotheism" to perfect the world can be transmitted through the agency of "Universal Zionism," the State of Israel. Of particular relevance to the proposal made below is the following from the concluding chapter: "For Jews to transform the world, then, we must first transform ourselves, from a community of individuals into a collective entity comfortable in the community of nations. Then, and only then, can the Jewish people fulfill their destiny."[9]

The Consensus

A most interesting aspect of the above analyses is the consensus that solutions have to be found by rebuilding the younger generations of Israelis from within and by remaining dedicated to traditional values. This is significant because, for the first sixty years of the state's existence, the approach had been to look outside, banking the state's identity and future on the search for peace. That approach did not achieve the desired goal; in fact, the opposite happened. In the last decade, Israel experienced broader criticism and wider hatred. This thirty-year experiment showed that when the nation focuses on its enemies, it will forget that its survival depends on its own citizens.

Fundamental, long-term questions had been ignored for two generations: Who are we? What is our unique historical role? Can Jews be more than the victims of the Holocaust? How does the State of Israel shape a Jewish future if it is not exclusively Jewish? As a consequence, how

---

9 Ian Pear, *The Accidental Zionist: What a Priest, a Pornographer and a Wrestler Named Chainsaw Taught Me about Being Jewish, Saving the World and Why Israel Matters to Both* (Jerusalem: New Song Publishers, 2008), 247.

different should the State of Israel be in relation to other states, including those that Israelis admire?

These issues are no less existential than the pursuit of peace. Even more, addressing these fundamental questions opens a path to addressing the external issues of peace and global anti-Israel hatred.

Proposed Solution: Eliminating Hatred by Building *Arevut*

Disclaimer

The first step should be a disclaimer about interference in Israeli matters by a Diaspora Jew. It is the same as that articulated by nationally syndicated radio talk show host and author Dennis Prager: "I do not believe it is the business of any American Jew to tell a mature democracy faced with threats to its existence what policies it should follow. Living in the safety of America, 10,000 miles away, I won't tell you – whose lives are on the line every day – what you should do."[10] Mr. Prager explains further that a disclaimer is not needed when one is not discussing "policy matters." This is the case here, since the proposal below is at the level of the individual, not the government.

There are two other reasons why the proposal articulated in this book does not need a disclaimer:

1. In 2010, a new Jewish world order was developing where the distinction between Diaspora Jews and Israelis was diminishing. The disappearance of support of Israel by the international community had a significant impact on Diaspora Jewry. The latter lost the freedom to remain aloof to Israel's challenges. The impetus for this change originated from unexpected sources: it came from young Arabs in Parisian suburbs who treated French Jews as if they were

10 Dennis Prager, "An Open Letter to Israel's Jews," *Jewish Journal*, June 15, 2010.

directly responsible for Operation Cast Lead in Gaza. It came from young Muslims in London who intentionally blurred the lines between British Jew and Israeli. As explained in the previous chapter, the tendency to link all Jews to the political or military actions of the State of Israel became omnipresent on United States campuses.

As a result, Diaspora Jews could no longer hide behind their non-Israeli passports. The new motto was "the Jews are Israel, and Israel the Jews." This "unification" of Jews was also echoed by Israeli writers: "Therefore, Israeli Jews and Jews in the Diaspora have a decision to make. They can capitulate before their enemies and give up the battle to stay alive, or they can decide that the Jewish people has not come this far to fail now."[11] This newfound Jewish unity has a built-in irony: with its hatred, the Muslim world wished to expel Israelis and to turn them back into Diaspora Jews, but it succeeded in achieving the opposite, turning Diaspora Jews into Israelis.

2. Because the proposal below is about baseless hatred, it involves all Jews, not just Israelis. Its implementation requires an ongoing dialogue between Diaspora and Israeli Jews and this does not constitute interference in the State of Israel's policies.

Proposal: Vision and Rationale

The time has come for the Jewish people (Israel and Diaspora) to address the issue of *sinat hinam* (baseless hatred) among Jews and its antidote, *arevut* (mutual responsibility). As described in chapter 4, there is a deep historical precedent that all Jews are bound to each other by an obligation of mutual responsibility called *arevut*. The notion of *arevut* preceded the formation of the Jewish peoplehood. It is authentically rooted in Jewish

---

11 Gordis, *Saving Israel*, 217.

history as part of a people-land paradigm and is therefore at the core of Jewish national identity. Taking responsibility for the well-being of others is what joins Jews into a single unit. It has been compared to a "cement" that binds Jews together, wherever they may be. It is an essential component of Jewish identity that is vulnerable to any type of internal hatred.

The proposal to build *arevut* on a global scale is distinct and independent from Jewish unity that depends on external events generally initiated by enemies of Jews, as has occurred from time to time throughout Jewish history. Externally based unity has been described as "a unity imposed, as it were, from outside," because "from within, in terms of its own self-understanding, the Jewish people evinces no answering solidarity. External crisis unites Jews; internal belief divides. But that cannot be the basis of an enduring sense of peoplehood."[12] Externally based unity is temporary. The current proposal begins to build solidarity from within by eradicating baseless hatred from each Jew's heart and eventually arrives at a moral society.

Although the present proposal strives for national *arevut*, it is neither a political program nor a mythic vision. It is aimed at individual Jews and relies on their wisdom and willingness. Each person can achieve mutual responsibility by training the capacities of his or her advanced neural system to develop empathy in order to see the humanity of other Jews and the uniqueness of each individual. As shown further in chapter 10, empathy is achievable. Within the State of Israel, the logic of this *arevut* proposal is that unity leads to morality and morality leads to peace: after the Jews eliminate baseless hatred, will the rest of the world continue to hate them without cause?

---

12 Sacks, *One People*, viii.

Consistent with the State's History

In chapter 5, the case was made that the creation of the State of Israel offered a historic opportunity to create not just a Jewish state but a new Jewish people. The state had built a framework of institutions ideal for the development of *arevut*, including ancestral land, a unique language, a national army, a distinctive calendar (Jewish holidays) and access to Jerusalem, a city that fosters unity and togetherness. As discussed in chapter 5, the process of building a united people was derailed in the last thirty years by several factors, particularly the focus on external peace, which yielded divisiveness. The proposed moral paradigm would change the emphasis in Israel from land to people and continue the unfinished task of building a united and moral people.

Addresses Internal Issues Facing the State of Israel

Daniel Gordis made the following four statements (mentioned in the previous chapter) describing issues that must be addressed urgently:

1. "For the Jewish state to survive, Israelis need to recover a sense of purpose."[13]

2. "They must ask how they want Israel to be unique, different from other countries they nonetheless admire."[14]

3. "Israelis need to wrestle with the question of how the Jewish state should be Jewish."[15]

4. "The purpose of the Jewish state is to transform the Jews."[16]

The proposed moral paradigm addresses all four issues – the need for

---

13 Gordis, *Saving Israel*, 82.

14 Ibid.

15 Ibid., 218.

16 Ibid., 216.

purpose, the uniqueness, Jewishness, and personal transformation – and it does so with precision and specificity. Parenthetically, Rabbi Jonathan Sacks recently made an identical assessment when he wrote: "Jews, whether in Israel or elsewhere, need to recover a sense of purpose."[17]

The Nobel Prize winner Aaron Ciechanover lamented the lack of leaders able to be in charge of the country's spiritual affairs. The present proposal addresses this issue using a different avenue: it relies on the individual. It addresses the base of the pyramid because leaders change but the Jewish people remain. Also, people who decide to become moral individuals will undoubtedly produce moral leaders.

Caroline Glick proposed the mission of setting an example of loyalty to traditions of valor and human decency. The present *arevut* moral paradigm addresses these issues by setting an example of brotherhood and sisterhood and by showing that it is possible to care for others on a national scale.

Natan Sharansky described a mosaic society; the proposed moral paradigm is consistent with different communities living as distinct groups because each individual is linked to every other Jew whether or not he or she belongs to the same sub-group. These communities need not dissolve. Unity does not imply uniformity, otherwise how could one explain that upon leaving Egypt and entering Israel, the Jewish people were divided into twelve tribes? The mosaic vision of Natan Sharansky can be realized based on the choice of each individual to belong to a national yet tightly knit fabric.

The Universal Zionism of Rabbi Pear also places emphasis on personal transformation. The proposed moral paradigm is consistent with that vision and provides a specific approach to transformation (the next two chapters give a step-by-step process for individual Jews).

---

17 Sacks, *Future Tense*, 4.

The proposed moral paradigm also tackles the thorny issue of religion, including individuals who have an "antipathy to religious ritual," in Daniel Gordis's formulation. The moral paradigm has religious roots (as described in chapter 2) but does not involve specific religious ritual. Any individual who seeks a moral raison d'être for the State of Israel can participate following his or her own degree of attachment to religion. The issue of religion is discussed in more detail in the next chapter, dealing with methodology.

Addresses External Issues Facing the State

In chapter 6, it was proposed that Palestinian opposition was not about land but about Islamists' view of Jewishness. In chapter 7, the different analyses showed that Western nations are obsessed with "the Palestinians, and not the Chechens, the Tibetans, the Bosnians, the Tutsis, or the Sudanese" simply because the Palestinian Arabs are affected by the actions of Israelis. For those critics, any distinction between Jews and any other group in Israel becomes a form of apartheid and victimization at the hands of Jews. Do they have unrealistically high expectations of Jewish behavior?

Hatred is one of the world's most pressing problems. As an expert source attests, "Hate unquestionably has the potential to blow apart the evolving globalized world system."[18] Nevertheless, world leaders have not come up with a plan to address it except through warfare. But focusing on fighting acts of terrorism and violence comes too late in the process: the goal should be to address the feelings of hate that lead to violence. We must address the cause and not just the symptoms of this worldwide malady. Jews can have a role in this global equation since they have a strong tradition of recognizing the seriousness of hatred.

---

18 Dozier, *Why We Hate*, 30.

The proposed moral paradigm will also help Jews address the recent display of global hatred toward them and the resulting feelings of isolation. Global hatred would have no power to create self-doubt among Jews who are secure and aware of the hatred trap. These individuals already know what devastation hatred can wreak. They also know that hatred lasts and spreads easily. They will not respond to the non-Jewish world simply by hating them back, because they subscribe to the sage Hillel's "golden rule," articulated two thousand years ago: "That which is hateful to you, do not do to others." Jews will understand that acceptance and respect by other nations will eventually come when the latter will see that the Jews have used their freedom and sovereignty to become moral individuals. At that point, antisemitic voices that accuse Israel of being a terrorist or outlaw state will have no echo and will be silenced.

Consistent with Herzl's Vision

In his article, Natan Sharansky explained that Herzl's vision was that once Jews have a state, i.e., a national home, the root cause of antisemitism would disappear. However, as Sharansky details, "Even after a national home was established, however, Herzl's prophecy of an end to anti-Semitism went unfulfilled."[19] Herzl's vision to create a national home succeeded, even if recognition of Israel by the nations is still questioned. The younger generations of Jews have the responsibility to extend Herzl's vision and give his dream permanence, which they can do through the proposed moral paradigm. It is appropriate to emphasize again that this can be done by all Jews, independent of degree of religious commitment.

Diaspora Jews Must Be Involved

As mentioned at the outset, the proposal to build a moral society based

---

19   Sharansky, "The Political Legacy of Theodor Herzl," 87.

on mutual responsibility involves all Jews. The previous paragraphs focused mostly on the State of Israel based on its significance in Jewish destiny and the unique daily challenges that Israeli Jews face to avoid baseless hatred. However, Diaspora Jews also need to free themselves from the trap of baseless hatred. When they will, their families, communal institutions, and communities will be positively transformed. All the methods described in the next chapter are applicable to them even if their challenges may be less complex than those encountered by Israelis. One positive outcome for Diaspora Jews is that they will automatically feel at one with the Israeli people.

A Personal "Holocaust Remembrance"

As outlined in the previous chapter, the philosopher Alain Finkielkraut explained that some Western intellectuals and politicians engage in criticism of Israel to resolve their repressed guilt about the Holocaust. They purge their dark past when they are able to condemn Israel: if they can claim that Israel behaves shamefully, they feel relieved of shame for their own personal and collective misdeeds.

In the context of the analyses of hatred presented in this book and the proposed moral paradigm, it is appropriate (but risky) to point out why guilt about the Holocaust is not just German but broader in scope. After the end of World War II, the whole world uncovered the duplicitous methods used by the Nazis. Their system of war, victory, occupation, search for Jews, and transport of Jews in country after country confronted the populations of multiple European countries (Poland, the occupied area of the former USSR, Romania, Hungary, Czechoslovakia, France, Germany, Austria, Lithuania, Holland, Latvia, Belgium, Yugoslavia, Greece, Bulgaria, Denmark, Estonia, Norway, and Luxembourg) with a horrible choice: they had to either collaborate with the occupier or risk their lives.

We know that many did the latter since all Holocaust museums have
sections honoring "righteous gentiles" who risked their lives and those of
their families to protect Jews. But the shame of having to collaborate is
difficult to forget. When the veil was lifted and the information collated,
the world was shocked to realize that the Jews had been subjected to an
unprecedented multinational synergy of hatred. That guilt leads many
intellectuals to adopt the cause of the Palestinian Arabs and promote
them as victims of the Holocaust victims. Independent of the fact that
Holocaust memorials and museums should address this defilement of
Holocaust victims on a global scale, the proposed *arevut* paradigm offers
a personal avenue to respond to such attacks. With a renewed dedication
of *arevut*, each Jew commits to a different "never again" formula, one to
"never again" subject other Jews to hatred. This can become a personal
remembrance of the Holocaust.

Deep Roots in Jewish History

Connecting Israel's present and future to its history is essential. In
his analysis of Herzl's legacy and of the early history of the State of
Israel, Natan Sharansky described how Russian immigrants had come
to Israel in search of their roots but found that Jewish history had been
truncated, leading them to believe that anything significant started in
1948. In his opinion, that approach (used in the early years) had negative
consequences also for later generations of Israelis. Even more recently,
Ambassador Dore Gold published an analysis entitled "The Challenge to
Israel's Legitimacy" in which he showed that one approach utilized by
Israel's enemies is to deny any historic connection between the Jewish
people and the Land of Israel.[20] Therefore, any plan to build a model
moral society in Israel must be rooted in Jewish history.

Chapter 4 traced the history of the concept of *arevut* throughout Jewish

20   Gold, "The Challenge to Israel's Legitimacy," 3.

history. Judah, the prototype Jew in Israel, introduced the notion of mutual responsibility by putting his life at risk for his brother and established the link between the Land of Israel and mutual responsibility. The concept of *arevut* was ratified at the covenant of Sinai and also when the Jewish people entered the Land of Israel. The importance of mutual responsibility continued to be emphasized throughout Jewish history, until the year 68 CE when the "one people=one land" equation was manifested. The 1,878-year exile that ensued delivered the message that the Land of Israel was given to a people, not to a group of individuals. Whenever Jews do not form a "cemented" people, they do not need (deserve) the land. Jewish unity is an inner "title" to the land that cannot be externally challenged. Now, after the end of the nineteen-century physical exile and sixty-two years of existence of the State of Israel, the Jewish people must reestablish its commitment to mutual responsibility to be consistent with its history and embrace its destiny on its land.

9

How to Prevent Baseless Hatred

The previous chapter described a proposal to respond to the new reality of global hatred or isolation through dedication to mutual responsibility and the elimination of baseless hatred among Jews everywhere. These last two chapters describe an implementation plan for this new moral paradigm that does not require any type of formal organization or infrastructure. The plan depends on the willingness of individual Jews to do the following four things:

1. To save themselves and their families from the disease of hatred

2. To enhance their lives by eliminating the destructive consequences of hatred

3. To connect with others in a caring and supportive way

4. To achieve a personal victory over themselves and over human nature in general

Each person is free to either choose inertia (to continue to react to situations as they come) or to take on the individual challenge of combating hatred. Experts agree that there is no known magic bullet cure for hatred. But there are a number of specific steps that can be used successfully to curb hatred and its consequences. This chapter presents methods to prevent new episodes while the next chapter focuses on repairing existing hatred relationships.

Preventing Hatred: Know Your Personal "Hatred Map"

Hatred is a response to a trigger, real or perceived. To succeed in preventing it, we need to focus on its emergence and its intensity. Hatred emerges quickly, sometimes even without our awareness. It sneaks up on you without warning. Its intensity depends on the type of trigger, the personality characteristics of the recipient, and the previous relationship between the two parties. Prevention of new episodes can be achieved by learning to recognize potential triggers and by understanding the personality factors that make a person hypersensitive.

At first glance, it would seem that the sources of hate triggers are infinite since they arise in a multitude of situations: public, private (home, family encounters), social or business (workplace) interactions. It also seems that hatred would be "impossible" to control because we cannot predict the behaviors of others toward us, and therefore we cannot predict how we will react. Such assessments are misleading and false. We can develop a different, proactive attitude based on an understanding of relationships most likely to produce hate triggers. That can be achieved by viewing ourselves at the center of a series of emotional concentric circles where each circle includes individuals with whom we have emotional links, such as siblings, parents, in-laws, extended family members, neighbors, coworkers, and friends. Those individuals constitute our personal potential hatred map, and we will analyze them as possible sources of hate triggers.

Siblings

The closest circle includes siblings: brothers and sisters. As we saw in the introduction and in chapter 4, siblings have natural tendencies to compete and many opportunities to do so. They tend to compare their status with each other implicitly or explicitly, whether or not it is realistic and sometimes to the point of obsession.

Scenario 9.1: Who Gets the Jewelry?

Leah was an older woman who outlived her husband. When she passed away, she left an inheritance with vague instructions for equal division between her son, Naftali, and her daughter, Nehama. Naftali is married with six children, while Nehama has only one older daughter. Immediately after the week-long shiva period, at the suggestion of his wife, Naftali asks for a meeting with his sister to discuss estate division. He comes to the meeting with his wife, and at the outset, his wife brings up the notion that the needs of her family are greater than those of Nehama's because of the difference in family size. That comment is not well received by Nehama; she has always felt sensitive and deprived about the fact that she was not able to have more than one child. That comment creates a tense atmosphere but the discussion about division of assets proceeds.

The deal breaker comes when Nehama expresses her strong feeling that all of her late mother's jewelry should go to her and her daughter and that Naftali (and his wife) have no claim to them. At that point, the tone of the meeting changes drastically and the "discussion" degenerates into strong disagreements, no resolution on any issue, and, eventually, recourse to attorneys. The trust between Naftali and Nehama is lost and their relationship never recovers. They no longer spend holidays together and the relationships between cousins also disintegrate.

Relationships between siblings can be very fragile. They are complicated by a multiplicity of factors, some of which may be hidden, and may date back to events that took place during childhood. Therefore, in principle, siblings should exercise extra care to avoid disagreements and arguments. The wise person should be proactive: knowing that these relationships are fragile, siblings should protect their bonds and strengthen them through mutual respect and expressions of support. One effective way to achieve this objective is to refrain from speaking negatively about any sibling in private or in public.

Parents

The next circle includes one's parents. Although they are not peers, relationships between parents and adult children can be quite complex because of long histories of emotional ties. As they grow older, children become independent and tend to become distant from their parents in order to assume their own spousal relationships and build their families. In that process, some adult children transport with them negative childhood memories or resentments (sometimes baseless) that they store for decades. Thus, even a normal evolution toward maturity can create the potential for adult children to manifest diminished tolerance toward their parents. As a result, innocuous words or criticisms by parents can trigger strong reactions from adult children.

Although parents tend to be more forgiving than children, and children are commanded "Honor your father and mother," parents should not assume that their adult children will do so. Wise parents who seek long-term peaceful relationships should adjust their approach to their children as they become adults. In particular, parents should avoid bringing up old negative images or memories from childhood. They should also avoid speaking negatively about one child to another.

Similarly, adult children should not "turn the page" on their parents just because they are involved in building their own lives and achieving professional success. Also, they should refrain from the temptation of constantly judging their parents, especially about events that took place decades before. Those judgments can be unjust and trigger unnecessary pain. (Parenthetically, peace between parents and children is given unique importance by Jewish tradition, which considers it to be one of the ultimate achievements of Elijah the prophet at the end of times.)

Cousins, Uncles, Aunts

The next circle includes extended family members such as cousins, uncles, and aunts. Cousins tend to consider each other as peers. When they are the same sex and age and live in close proximity, competitiveness among cousins may sneak in even from a young age. Cousins, like siblings, have an implicit tendency to compare their status and achievements with each other simply because their parents are siblings (that may seem absurd, but it takes place subconsciously). Although there is less affection for a cousin than a sibling, these relationships should not be taken for granted because negative attitudes can develop rapidly and are difficult to repair.

Uncles and aunts are not considered peers and may feel a little more distant because of age, but they also tend to compare their nephews and nieces to their own children. For example, during family gatherings, it is not unusual for an uncle or aunt to ask a nephew or niece, "So, did you find a job?" or "When will you get married? Still no one is good enough?" Such situations are classic traps, especially if the nephew or niece has already heard the same invasive inquiries before, where they are not addressed with care, sensitivity, and privacy. Adult nephews or nieces should try to answer without disrespect. Relationships with uncles and aunts may include other complicating factors: any tension between an aunt and her sister or brother, for example, will tend to carry over to the children of that sibling.

This is why family gatherings can turn into hatred traps. When individuals are not careful, these gatherings include fewer and fewer family members as time goes on.

In-Laws

In-laws are among the most critical sets of family peers in the series of emotional circles related to potential hatred. All in-laws are included: brother- or sister-in-law, father- or mother-in-law, and son- or daughter-in-law. In-laws are special because they are "acquired" peers, meaning that they enter into relationships with each other later in life, and not always as a result of free choice. For example, a man and woman decide to marry and their parents and siblings "inherit" in-law relationships. Therefore, it is easy to view in-laws as individuals who "disturb" an established family order. One basic problem pertains to the way in which our primitive neural system labels these new arrivals in the family.

Scenario 9.2: Ari's "Stupid" Brothers-in-Law

Scenario 9.2.1: *Ari, our main character, has a sister, Hannah, who is married to Ofir. Ari finds his new brother-in-law, Ofir, "stupid" because most of the time, Ofir jokes about family members and family situations and makes remarks that Ari finds inappropriate. Ofir thinks he is funny, especially when he is among his family, but Ari does not think so. Ari does not relate at all to his sense of humor. Ari wonders why his sister Hannah decided to marry Ofir and has always felt "stuck with" him. Ari avoids attending his sister's family events, which creates pressure in his sister's marriage.*

Scenario 9.2.2: *Ari is married to Malka, whose brother is Tzvi. Ari finds this other brother-in-law, Tzvi, also "stupid," but for different reasons. Tzvi is not married; he is younger than Ari but is not respectful toward him. Ari believes that Tzvi was raised spoiled, without having to make an effort to earn a living. Here also, Ari considers himself "stuck with" Tzvi because Malka happens to have a "stupid" brother.*

In the first case, Ari feels stuck with Ofir because, subconsciously, he refuses to accept that his sister Hannah can make a decision that does not suit him. Ari refuses to admit that for Hannah, Ofir is a wonderful husband. Deep inside, Ari considers that his bond to his sister is a tool and that he should be able to fashion his environment in his own image. This type of self-centered and irrational expectation and the feeling of being trapped are typical of an insecure person chronically under the control of his primitive neural system. Yet Ari is a very successful school principal.

In the second case, it has escaped Ari that Tzvi was Malka's brother before he ever met Malka. If he feels stuck with Tzvi, it is principally because of his choice to marry Tzvi's sister. Ari is oblivious to his own responsibility and sees Tzvi as a problem that he inherited. Ari believes that Malka's family mishandled their wealth in raising their children and that her family is "inferior" to his own. Ari thinks (and sometimes states) that he would have been better off had his wife come from a different family. Never does Ari adjust to the fact that he is in a situation that he created, thus illustrating a clear case of misplaced causality. Also he does not realize that he might be jealous of Tzvi's wealth. His overall attitude and the fact that he feels "stuck" are signatures of a primitive neural system that needs to be readjusted.

In both cases, Ari could solve these issues by (1) realizing that he is a member of the family, not its center; (2) accepting Ofir and Tzvi as they are; and (3) understanding that their behavior is outside of his zone of control and that he is a victim of no one except himself.

A very potent in-law conflict was seen in scenario 1.2, in which Sarah's mother in-law made a comment about her wedding dress on the wedding night. Let's add some additional context to the situation: when Avi was dating Sarah, Avi's mother was not in favor of the wedding. Sarah eventually found out and when Avi finally married Sarah, Sarah felt vindicated but never forgot her mother in-law's initial attitude. When her mother in-law made a negative comment about her wedding dress, Sarah had already reached zero tolerance because that night she had achieved final victory: the wedding was proceeding and she felt that her mother in-law should no longer have any influence on the new couple. This is why, even twenty years later, at the mother in-law's seventieth birthday celebration, Sarah remembered the wedding night comment vividly, to her husband's amazement. The perpetuation of the original offense intact in her memory for decades and her vindictive attitude are typical by-products of the primitive neural system.

Another example of a strained in-law relationship is seen in our next scenario.

Scenario 9.3: Tzippy and Rachel

Tzippy is a mother who has a strong bond with her son Zvulun, who just married Rachel. In the first year following the wedding, Rachel expresses her discomfort with the close links between her husband and his mother (multiple phone calls per day), which she finds childish. Rachel feels that Zvulun should develop new allegiances toward her (eventually including their children). Furthermore, immediately after the wedding, Rachel decided to call her mother in-law by her first name (Tzippy), which was not appreciated by the latter. Thus, the mother in-law and daughter in-law were "thrown into" a competing relationship, as if they were peers.

The daughter in-law, Rachel, feels that she is "stuck" with her husband's mother, who is unable to evolve from her past relationship with her son. The mother in-law, Tzippy, feels that this situation was "imposed" on her by her son Zvulun's "wrong" choice. Here, both Tzippy and Rachel see each other as an imposition. These assessments are fueled by their primitive neural systems, which provide them with justifications to resist a cooperative and peaceful relationship.

Relationships among in-laws are naturally ripe for the generation of hatred for several reasons. The most common danger comes from the "us versus them" divisions. The built-in challenge comes from the fact that men and women are attracted by someone "different" as opposed to the people they grew up with (who are not as "interesting"). As a result, when they decide to get married, more often than not, they bring together two families with different styles and approaches. These families feel fine as they are and not ready to change or adopt different values.

As soon as discussions about wedding plans start, stark differences emerge. The smallest details take on gigantic proportions: who will walk in what order, theme colors of dresses and flowers, type of band and music. Other troublesome issues are the number of guests coming from each side and the seating arrangements for each set of guests. The danger of damaged relationships increases when a disagreement surfaces about who will pay for a particular item. All these issues can permanently affect future rapport between the families. The situation is particularly dangerous for the future husband and wife, since all these differences appear early in their relationship, before they have had a chance to strengthen their emotional bonds. The newlyweds end up "paying for" the fact that the two families have different values. That creates unnecessary pain and is avoidable.

These facts are well known, yet we seem to stumble over them time and again. Here are some suggested solutions for the parents:

1. Recognize that relationships between in-laws intrinsically involve competing interests; they are a minefield and must be approached with the utmost care.

2. Weigh the reason for any disagreement.

3. If you are not willing to compromise, re-examine one more time why.

4. If you compromise, do it for your kids; it is a worthwhile investment in their life with a new partner.

5. Stop the "us versus them" distinctions, which are unfair because they lump people together and ignore individuality.

6. Avoid negative gossip about the in-laws because they are your new family.

7. Remember that it is not about you; it is not your wedding.

Workplace

After family members, coworkers are important members of our personal hatred maps or emotional circles because we are compelled to have frequent encounters and because the workplace is a competitive environment. This is particularly the case in a time such as the present, when there is uncertainty about job stability and the global economy. Workers know that their jobs depend on the competitiveness of their companies, but they can do little to alter these external factors, so they feel like victims. This leads to anxiety and stress, and sometime frustration and dissatisfaction. Examples of potentially negative work-related situations include resentment of a worker toward another who performs better or frustration with superiors or managers because they are responsible for evaluations and upward mobility. Some individuals may resent their bosses even after they leave their jobs.

There are cases of anger that turns into full-blown hatred when a worker loses his or her job. In the United States, this phenomenon has lead to workplace shootings where an employee who was fired came back and started shooting randomly at former coworkers. This occurs because the primitive neural system perpetuates the memory of the original offense indefinitely. One must be aware of the potential pitfalls of the workplace, especially at the beginning of one's career. Competition can exist and must be handled in a wise way. Growth in an organization or in one's business is based on the ability to learn from others, to accept criticism, and to be patient. All of these require a good control of one's emotions and particularly one's insecurities.

Neighbors

Similar to coworkers, neighbors are individuals with whom we have competing interests and frequent encounters and who cannot be easily avoided. Neighbors live parallel lives and share many experiences but they may not share the same values. In some cases, lifestyles are different and neighbors end up imposing them on one another. In other cases, there are situations where neighbors share common facilities or resources. All of these situations include multiple opportunities for friction. Misunderstandings may arise for the smallest reasons: we may not appreciate the way neighbors leave their garbage cans or occupy the elevator or make noise at night or abuse their share of the parking space. One family may feel that the children of another have awful manners and preclude the children from socializing.

In these cases, even when one side tries to dialogue, they encounter a wall of resistance. Disagreements lead to arguments because each side is convinced of the correctness of their position. Some neighbors become "allergic" to each other and engage in long-term retaliation. One will plant a tree or build a new section of their home in order to block the view of the other, and the other will retaliate by making more noise at night. When they meet, they do not talk to each other or even offer a simple greeting; they express their anger or hatred by a look or a smirk. Ultimately, they have recourse to attorneys to enforce what they believe are their rights. These situations are very ripe for the "us versus them" mentality and the development of hatred. Each side then considers the other an enemy. These situations are difficult to reverse or repair (see below).

This type of behavior may be related to modern living but it is not part of Jewish heritage. The standards of Jewish dwelling were set long ago while the Jews were wandering in the desert. The non-Jewish prophet Balaam could not help but praise the Jewish people for the rules they used to set up thousands of tents in a camp and still avoid intruding on each other's privacy.[1] The entrance of each tent was arranged to avoid facing another so that each family had no worry about voyeurism. There were no smirks or bad looks. This type of sensitivity to privacy was unprecedented and set mutual respect as the Jewish standard of dwelling together.

Friends

Most individuals have a circle of friends. Unlike family members, coworkers or neighbors, these are not individuals with whom we are compelled to have frequent encounters since, in principle, friends are chosen. Nevertheless, friendship is a complex phenomenon, often

---

1   This is found in Numbers 24:5.

misunderstood. Friendship is not simply based on mutual interests or similarity of hobbies. Ideally, it is a relationship where both parties express empathy, honesty, and understanding, and each seeks what is best for the other. True friendship should be altruistic, if it is to be sustained.

But because friends share some intimacy, common characteristics (age, orientation), and interests, they constitute peers. If they are not very careful, they will tend to use each other as yardsticks, comparing their status (economic, professional, family) with each other. That may feel natural but it is a trap because they may become unable to rejoice for each other's successes. Relationships among "friends" can become polluted by competition, envy, or even jealousy. Then, instead of providing support, such individuals rejoice internally when their "friends" have a setback. When this occurs, those relationships become superficial and are not easy to maintain.

Some of the serious dangers of friendships are expectations that are unspoken and unrealistic. In chapter 2, scenario 2.1, Reuven had assumed he was a "friend" of the Cohens and expected to be invited to their son's wedding. When he was not invited, he was not just disappointed. He did not forget about it, and did not forgive them. Later, when his own daughter was about to get married, he initially decided to retaliate and not invite the Cohens.

In chapter 1, we discussed scenario 1.1, "The Full Plate." Shimon could have been a "good friend" of Reuven's and made the remark about Reuven's full plate as a teasing joke. Nevertheless, Reuven was offended, because when we feel insecure, we implicitly seek validation from friends. Most people do not enjoy being mocked, and especially not by the very people to whom they turn for approval. True friends should realize that their friends need and expect support and above all respect from them.

Detecting and Countering Hatred Triggers within the Personal Map

Prevention of hatred becomes possible if we develop early detection and alert systems based on knowledge of (1) one's personal map (as outlined above) and (2) the functioning of the primitive and advanced neural systems, which will be reviewed very briefly here.

In chapter 1, we learned about the primitive neural system, which is also called our primitive mind or our reptomammalian mind. It includes multiple structures in our inner brain, and specifically refers to the amygdala, which evaluates the information received from our senses for any sign of threat or pain. The advanced neural system is located in the outer area of the brain, called the cerebral cortex, and is capable of sophisticated functions such as interpretation, reflection, conceptualization, foresight, and particularly our capacity for empathy toward others.

The primitive and advanced neural systems are connected through the limbic association cortex (orbitofrontal cortex) and compete for the control of our thoughts, emotions, and behavior. The amygdala labels the information it receives from the sensory systems in a primitive way (as either positive or negative) that is difficult to alter. The orbitofrontal cortex is far more complex and malleable: it stores our general knowledge of how the world works. The neocortex, a part of the cerebral cortex, uses information contained in the orbitofrontal cortex to counter the primitive neural system's snap-judgment classifications.

The usefulness of this differentiation is to understand that we can, for example, experience an unpleasant social interaction and mislabel it as a threat based on our insecurities. Our goal is to learn how to use our higher brain functions to stop the primitive neural system from unnecessarily categorizing our interactions as threatening. By consciously activating the higher analytical functions of the cerebral cortex, we can avoid reactions that lead to hatred.

Most of us are not always aware of how insecure or competitive (or even envious) we might be toward specific family members or friends or coworkers. Awareness of our personal hatred map helps us realize that our sensitivity toward those individuals may be exaggerated. Therefore, we can act proactively by being more careful with those individuals.

To help us in that effort, we should reflect on the notion of ego: How secure or self-confident are we? The degree to which we will tolerate a perceived assault from a member of our map depends on our ego – that is, on our sense of self. When the ego is in balance, a person has a realistic understanding of his own importance and a healthy sense of self-confidence. The more we succeed in that direction, the more tolerant we will be. The converse is true. Insecure individuals tend to compensate for their low self-esteem by inflating their egos – ironically, a poor self-image tends to result in an inflated sense of one's own importance. That is the other end of the spectrum and it is what we wish to avoid.

A general principle of interactions with members of one's map is that words that create the smallest discomfort provoke negative emotions that are registered by the primitive neural system as threatening and therefore run the risk of developing into hatred. We should train our higher analytical brain functions to override this reaction; whenever we hear upsetting words from a member of our personal map, before reacting to any perceived assault, we should instantly trigger reflex questions such as the following:

- Am I envious or jealous of this person?
- Am I insecure? Why?
- Does this person make me insecure? Why?
- Does my self-esteem depend on others?

Also, if we receive a criticism we should not react until we determine whether it is valid, truly unfair, or just perceived as unfair. This "fairness" criterion is important because it determines our reaction. Recent studies have shown that "we get immediate satisfaction from punishing people who have behaved unfairly. We do not feel any empathy for the suffering of these undesirable people."[2] Similarly, we must learn to analyze any perceived threat and determine its impact: does it just affect my well-being at the moment or is it a threat only to my desires and ambitions? By involving our higher brain functions in this immediate self-questioning, we stop the primitive neural system from grabbing a perception and categorizing it as an assault without examination.

Let us assume that somehow those steps were not successful and we do feel hurt as a result of a remark by someone in our personal map. We must then tackle the next step, the emergence of hatred. To do so, we rely on the series of steps described in chapter 2. If you consider yourself a "victim" of an assault, then you should take the initiative to speak to the "aggressor" in a respectful way indicating that you are pursuing the matter only because he or she is important to you. The purpose of the discussion is to put the incident in perspective and realize its true dimensions. Most of the time, this is enough to demote the incident from its over-prominent status in our psyche and relegate it to its proper status as a minor event. If that happens, the situation is mostly resolved at the time.

Whether or not it is resolved, you should erase it from your memory to avoid keeping a grudge or, worse, planning a retaliatory move. The attitude should be: "If I do not resolve these minor issues as they come, after a while I will end up carrying an enormous amount of luggage containing all these hurts and ill feelings, each waiting for some retaliation!" Each of these pieces of luggage should have been "checked"

---

2 Frith, *Making Up the Mind*, 191.

at its counter at the moment it arose. Instead, you allowed them to turn into "carry-on," most of which is unnecessary. With excessive "carry-on" it becomes difficult to travel. A practical measure of success in this endeavor is whether, after the incident, we feel the urge to speak negatively about the person in question. If we do, then more internal work of forgiveness is needed.

A consequence of this mindset is the awareness of the chronic need to strengthen one's self-confidence. We must seek to free ourselves from relying on others to bolster our self-esteem. A well-kept secret about combating hatred is that freedom from dependence on others is not a result of rejecting them but of respecting them. At the same time, when we respect others we become more secure, less sensitive, and happier. In the end, goodness toward others ends up being good for oneself!

Understanding the Broader "Hatred Map"

The next circle is broad and not as well defined because it includes individuals and groups of individuals who belong to the larger societal environment and with whom we have rare interactions. Unlike the personal map, which is the same for people all over the world, this broad hatred map presents challenges that are very different in the Diaspora and in Israel.

Diaspora

Jews live in a variety of groups or communities more or less open or more or less homogeneous depending on the country. In every country, some Jews choose not to identify with any community and their broader map is reduced. Independent of the situation of any particular Jew, the broader map in the Diaspora is quite simple compared to that in Israel (see further). Jews who belong to the same community share institutions such as synagogues, schools, community centers, social organizations, and kosher restaurants. In the Diaspora, there are divisions between institutions at the macro level such as denomination (Orthodox, Conservative, Reconstructionist, Reform, Renewal, etc.) or at the level of traditions even among a given group (Sephardic versus Ashkenazic, Hasidic versus Mitnagdic). These unavoidable differences create the potential for prejudice and labeling: this is dangerous and unfair because all members of another denomination are stereotyped gratuitously and the significance of individual Jews disappears.

In each community, there are daily opportunities for social and business interactions that create the potential for hatred if they are not handled with care. In the life of any community, differences arise either between members or with their religious or lay leaders.

Differences between rabbi and members arise frequently because of unspoken and therefore unmet expectations. If a synagogue member becomes hospitalized and the rabbi did not pay a hospital visit, the consequences can become personalized: the formerly sick person and his or her family hold a grudge against the rabbi that can last for some time. Similarly, if the rabbi happens to be out of town the weekend of the wedding of the child of a prominent member, the rabbi may feel the consequences of his absence. In both cases, individuals had expected that the rabbi would be there "for them" in times of need. He was not and the reasons do not seem to matter.

Similarly, differences in opinion occur between lay members of institutional committees or boards or committees: even though the differences pertain to the direction of the organization, they can easily turn personal or political. All these can result in mistrust, bitterness, and fragmentation (for example, the creation of a breakaway synagogue or school). Usually lay leaders are volunteers with sincere intentions who deserve respect at least for their dedication. These types of disagreements tend to have personal consequences that are difficult to erase and greatly diminish the efficiency of the organization. However, they can be prevented (see below).

As above, each person involved in those activities should be alert to develop early detection and alert systems within this broader "hatred map." One starting point is to work on oneself to erase prejudice against other denominations or groups of Jews. A common trap one should seek to avoid is feeling superior, super-pious, or self-righteous, thus excluding large segments of the Jewish people. Nor should more overtly religious groups be dismissed as fanatics or extremists.

It pays to remember that the notion of peace (*shalom*) never implied uniformity but actually harmony among different groups who each have their uniqueness or singularity: the twelve *shevatim* (tribes) each had their own path and respected each other's different ways of serving God and their people. Zebulun never looked down on Issachar for "just learning," and Issachar never looked down on Zebulun for "just working" (see chapter 4). They each valued the other's contribution. We must also work on ourselves to learn to at least tolerate differences without feeling threatened.

One can also be proactive to avoid becoming emotionally involved in disputes with other Jews from the same institution. There are routine interpersonal exchanges that have an infinite number of triggers (example given in scenario 1.1). One member is moved by a style of prayer with a lot of singing while another may prefer a shorter prayer service. There is no way to resolve such a situation except for tolerance. Another classic example is the Jew coming to synagogue on a regular day and saying to another, "You are in my seat," even before saying "Hello." Experience has shown that large and bitter community rifts can arise from minute interpersonal disagreements.

Israel

The situation in Israel is different from that in the Diaspora, more complex by an order of magnitude simply because Israel is the national home of the Jews. We learned previously that home can be a very fertile ground for the emergence of competition, rivalry, and resentment because interactions are with individuals with whom we have strong emotional ties. For that reason, negative interactions can produce more hurt, perhaps because we are more sensitive and because we naturally have higher expectations of family members. It is also at home that we assert our self-confidence, which can also contribute to impatience and sometimes intolerance.

The same phenomena take place at the level of a society, particularly the Israeli society, which to some extent functions as a large family. For example, some Israelis feel that since Israel is a large family, they implicitly expect every other citizen to have high standards of behavior.

Israeli society presents unique challenges based on its historical heterogeneity since its citizens came from numerous countries with different lifestyles and customs. This leads to the existence of stereotypes, labels, and categorizations based on superficial criteria, creating multiple and complex issues. In what follows, we list a few that have been associated with profound divisions (called "fault lines"). Here, we are only interested in the facets related to curbing baseless hatred.

Land. "Nothing causes more heated debate among Israelis than the quarter of a million of their fellow citizens who live among three and a half million Palestinians."[3] This refers to the more than 120 settlements throughout the West Bank. This phenomenon is divisive because it

---

3   Donna Rosenthal, *The Israelis: Ordinary People in an Extraordinary Land* (New York: Free Press, 2003), 209.

reveals differences in fundamental beliefs: about religion, the Land of Israel, the path to peace, relationships with Palestinian Arabs, the role of the military, the right to protection from terrorism, and the ultimate safety of the State of Israel as a whole. Some settlement-related issues become instantaneously explosive, such as soldiers obeying orders from their rabbis rather than their army superiors. No society can be expected to have mechanisms to resolve such existential differences except for individual effort. That is why the proposals to build *arevut* made in these last two chapters depend on individuals.

Ethnic origin. Israel has been called one nation made of several "tribes." At the macroscopic level, there are Ashkenazim, Mizrahim, Sephardim, Russians, Ethiopians, and others, and each of these groups subdivides further into individual countries of origin and sometimes even further. In the previous chapter, we referred to the description of Natan Sharansky deploring "a society made up of distinct groups that tend to keep mostly to themselves, put sectarian interests above national ones, and compete for control of the country."[4] In the present context, all we propose is that ethnic origin per se should not be an issue; it becomes one only because of the interpretation we choose to give it.

Ethnic origin may be relevant to individual identity but it does not dictate behavior. Diversity is not fragmentation. From the moment of its creation, the Jewish people were divided into twelve tribes: as they left Egypt, Jews traveled the desert according to their tribes. When they arrived to the land of Canaan, the land was also divided according to the different tribes. There were divisions but they did not originally create divisiveness: the people understood then that peace does not imply uniformity but rather harmony among distinct groups. (Later in history tribal conflicts did occur but they were caused by self-serving interests of individuals.)

---

4 Sharansky, "The Political Legacy of Theodor Herzl," 87.

What is urgently needed is respect for the identity and uniqueness of different groups. Leading psychologists explain that prejudice toward a social group can be very subtle and yet include the seeds of hatred. It may manifest itself only as mild discomfort with no visible anger; the person nurses feelings of superiority, contempt, or disgust but these are not visible as open discrimination until they can be justified by some other factor such as behavior that we do not condone (the way they drive or the way they vote). But this is not inevitable. The development of hatred can be stopped at its inception, if people are aware of the potential for it and alert to situations that carry the potential to blossom into hatred.

In short, diversity does not have to be an impediment to Israeli unity; it can be turned into an asset for the country, especially if individuals show that they can overcome the traps of stereotypes.

Religion. The issue of religion has been called the "religious-secular divide" and is considered a widening fault line. It manifests itself in many ways. Israeli society is very clearly subdivided along religious lines, and the differences among groups are clearly visible based on the type and color of one's clothing, hairstyle, and head covering. Whether or not a person is religious is immediately apparent from his or her mode of dress. Within the religious public, both men and women can be more or less immediately typed based on their head covering alone. Whether a woman wears a scarf (and what type of fabric it is made of), a wig, or a hat over a wig makes it immediately clear to which group she belongs. Likewise a man's political and religious affiliation is evident in his choice of *kippa*: what color it is, and whether it is woven or leather or velvet, with or without a band around the rim of it, are all cues to his identity, to the extent that this unique science has been wryly dubbed "Kippology."[5]

---

5 Rosenthal, *The Israelis*, 229.

Areas of encounter between Jews with different degrees of religiosity include common public transportation. In those situations, external appearance and modesty (or lack thereof) in dress sometimes create friction. Even when these incidents occur they should not become the source for divisive stereotyping: we should not fall into the trap of seeing other Jews only through their attire, whether or not it is modest. More serious are the occasional confrontations about traffic on Shabbat: "During demonstrations to keep the street open to Shabbat traffic, sometimes police erect barriers to separate the ultra-Orthodox from the non-Orthodox...."[6] These types of situations are detrimental in many ways. Firstly, they tend to widen rather than bridge the religious gap. Secondly, they are publicized sometimes worldwide and promote the notion that Jews are unable to agree on the very thing that makes them Jewish, feeding Jew-bashers throughout the world.

The religious-secular divide is also visible at the urban level: Jerusalem is viewed by some as a religious city while Tel Aviv is considered secular (the same applies to Safed and Eilat). Some degree of separation within neighborhoods is understandable based on practical considerations and differences in services and infrastructure needed by religious and secular Jews. But we must hope that the religious-secular divide does not result in divisions at the national level. That would not be compatible with the vision of Israel as one moral nation.

A more visible and provoking example is the difference in attitude toward Yom Hazikaron, the Israeli equivalent of Memorial Day: "Shocking television scenes of yeshiva boys laughing or playing while the siren sounds infuriate most Israelis, who, for decades, have been accusing them of a massive draft dodge."[7] On one hand, such manifestations of

---

6 Ibid., 238.

7 Ibid., 202.

"in-your-face" challenges are painful and reveal deep failures of self-control and basic respect. On the other, those who publicize these images bear the responsibility of igniting fires and widening internal divisions on core issues such as Zionist ideology and the role of religion within the Jewish state.

Stereotypes. A chronic, serious, and lurking danger to unity in Israeli society is the tendency to stereotype individuals that belong to different groups. The risk associated with such behavior is that these stereotypes are often accompanied by prejudice. Prejudice has been defined as "an unfair negative attitude toward a social group or a person perceived to be a member of that group."[8] Experts indicate that "the seeds of hatred are present in even subtle contemporary forms of prejudice."[9]

Here also, the solution does not lie with some government program but with the conviction and strength of individuals who recognize that such attitudes and beliefs are essentially unfair and immoral. The essence of the issue is to control how we react to what we see and hear. It is useful to remember that the primitive neural system thrives on prejudice and stereotypes because it applies gross generalizations. The urge to react to the behavior of another group with discomfort or disgust or in a resentful way reflects the perception of a threat. Therefore, before reacting with prejudice we must analyze the "threat" and determine whether it is purely perception and perhaps not factual at all. Here also it is useful to ask oneself: Why am I threatened? Why is it that this group or person's behavior makes me insecure?

In chapter 5, we addressed the question "Is there something uniquely difficult about interactions between Jews?" We answered positively and reviewed a number of reasons: they care for each other and program

8 Sternberg, *The Psychology of Hate*, 212.

9 Ibid., 213.

themselves to think (falsely and arrogantly) that they are the "last Jew."

There are several consequences of such attitudes. One may be that the distinction between a "personal" and a "broader" hatred map may not apply to Jews: deep inside, Jews consider each other members of the same family. Therefore, in Israeli society every person belongs in the "personal hatred map." That becomes unrealistic, the map becomes too large and too heavy; society becomes a minefield. If everyone is part of one's personal map, each Israeli must be alert with everyone, not just family members. This hypersensitivity may be what led Rabbi Sacks to articulate that for Jews "internal belief divides."[10] The degree of divisiveness was expressed as follows: "Had it not been for the fact that Israel has, since its birth and for twenty years before, faced a set of common enemies, it might well have split apart along any of a number of fissures."[11]

Another consequence is a high degree of intolerance. The following insight appeared recently: "Jews have this obsession with rebuking each other in the hope that they'll change one another – always chasing that elusive dream of a 'united approach.' But if that hasn't succeeded in 5,000 years, why should it succeed now? The way I see it, we're better off trying to turn our disunity into a virtue."[12] How can we do that? By focusing on the main objectives: to build a moral society, to survive the assaults of physical and political enemies, to be creative and contribute to the world. As a result, the attitude should be not just to "tolerate" differences among Jews but to accept them and each other. That can come from realizing that the destination is common and the destiny indivisible.

---

10   Sacks, *One People*, viii.

11   Sacks, *Future Tense*, 170.

12   David Suissa, "In Praise of Disunity," *Jewish Journal*, June 15, 2010.

Let us also remember that "The purpose of the Jewish state is to transform the Jews"[13] and that "Jewish unity is a cause that is not advanced by the advocacy of one point of view over another. It demands the difficult but not impossible exercise of thinking non-adjectivally as a Jew: not as a member of this or that group, but as a member of an indivisible people."[14]

Religious Practice and Baseless Hatred

We discussed above the topic of religion in Israeli society, which brings up an important question: What is the relationship between religious practices and baseless hatred? This discussion has three aspects: (1) baseless hatred coexists with religious practice, (2) reasons why the two should not coexist, (3) what can be done about it.

Aside from empirical observation around us, we know that baseless hatred can coexist with religious practice from the sages who articulated the notion of baseless hatred. As pointed out in the introduction, they specifically identified the people whose behavior led to the destruction of the Second Temple as religious. The Talmud (*Yoma* 9b) contains the statement "But [during the time of] the Second Temple, we know that the people occupied themselves with Torah, *mitzvot*, and acts of kindness." We noted in chapter 4 the death of the twenty-four thousand students of Rabbi Akiva who did not put aside their differences but maintained rivalries. We described above the instances of Shabbat traffic confrontations and defiance of Yom Hazikaron.

There are many reasons to expect that religious practice should diminish the existence of baseless hatred based on the emphasis placed on this issue by sages of all ages. A very small selection is reproduced here.

---

13 Gordis, *Saving Israel*, 216.

14 Sacks, *One People*, x.

Regarding hurting others verbally: "We should not speak any word to an Israelite that will pain or distress him.... For the Torah was exceedingly particular about wrong inflicted with words, because this is something very hard for the heart of people to bear and a great many persons care more about this than about [being wronged] in matters of property."[15]

Regarding hatred in the heart: "The hatred of the heart is more serious than any open hatred, and the Torah warned against it more strongly... for the hatred of the heart causes great evils among people, so that every man's sword is against his brother [Ezekiel 38:21] and against his neighbor...and it is the worst and most utterly despicable quality in the eyes of every intelligent human being."[16]

Regarding the dangers of responding to an incident by going silent, the sages refer us to the classical example of the hatred of Avshalom toward his half brother Amnon. Avshalom was the son of King David and had a sister by the name of Tamar. Amnon devised a devious plan and disgraced Avshalom's sister, Tamar. Avshalom had a just reason to hate Amnon. But instead of speaking to Amnon to seek any type of resolution, Avshalom remained silent. Eventually, his hatred led him to kill Amnon, which resulted in his own death and in a civil war.[17]

Regarding the dangers of responding to an incident by seeking revenge: "A man should know and reflect that whatever happens to him, good or bad, is caused by the Eternal Lord, blessed be He, to occur to him; from a human hand, from a man's brother's hand, nothing can be without the will of the Eternal Lord, blessed be He. Therefore, should a man inflict suffering or a pain on him, let him know in his soul that his bad deeds

---

15 Rabbi Pinhas Halevi of Barcelona, *Sefer haHinnuch: Student Edition*, translated by Charles Wengrov (Jerusalem: Feldheim Publishers, 1992), *mitzvah* 338.

16 Ibid., *mitzvah* 238.

17 For more details, see II Shmuel 13:1–22.

were the cause, and the Eternal Lord (be He blessed) decreed this upon him; and let him not set his thoughts to take revenge from him. For the other is not the [primary] cause of his trouble, since it is sin that brought it about. As David (peace be with him) said, 'So let him curse, because the Lord has told him' (II Samuel 16:10): he attributed the matter to his sin, not to Shimi ben Gerah.... Moreover, there is another great benefit resulting from the precept: [it serves] to stop contention and remove hate from people's hearts. And when there is peace among people, the Eternal Lord grants them peace."[18]

Regarding the commandment "You shall love your fellow as yourself": "A person who loves another as himself will not steal from him, will not commit adultery with his wife, will not cheat him of goods or oppress him with words, will not move his boundary, and will not harm him in any way."[19]

Regarding the notion of "permitted hatred as a way to rebuke a sinner," Rabbi Nachum Amsel writes: "The Chazon Ish, who lived in the twentieth century, says that there is no mitzvah to hate Jews today and no mitzvah to even rebuke sinners today. Thus, this category of hate is not applicable today."[20]

Another reason to expect that religious practice should curb the existence of baseless hatred is that the latter creates impossible situations within a religious context. For example, the use of the prayer book becomes difficult since most prayers are written in the plural and are all-inclusive: a Jew who hates fellow Jews, when praying, would be asking that the

---

18 HaLevi, *Sefer haHinnuch, mitzvah* 241.

19 Ibid., *mitzvah* 243.

20 Amsel, *Jewish Encyclopedia*, 93. Rabbi Amsel also points out, regarding living in Israel as a practicing Jew, that "there is something unique about this land that makes it respond differently from any other soil in the world. It is the only land that responds physically to moral behavior." Ibid., 126.

prayers of his or her enemy be realized as well. A wise person faced with that situation would become aware of the awkwardness and end up asking: Why should I put myself in such a paradoxical situation? The wise course would be to work on forgiving or even to pray to become able to forgive. When a person prays repeatedly for something, that person can't help but eventually reflect: Is there anything that I can do to help realize my prayer? The person would then realize that indeed he or she can let go and forgive.

Other examples of incongruence include Yom Kippur as described in chapter 4. That special day offers the unique opportunity of pardon and forgiveness for sins. However, seeking forgiveness from God for a wrong done to another person is a fruitless avenue. Forgiveness can only be obtained directly from the wronged party. Here also, the wise person would use the opportunity provided by that day to forgive, obtain forgiveness, and seek a definitive resolution.

Why is it that in spite of all these warnings, baseless hatred and religious practice seem to coexist quite well? Simply because baseless hatred is powerful and insidious. Religious persons may not realize that hatred is a trap embedded in our inner brains. It cannot be curbed or diminished indirectly, as a by-product of religious practice. It must be tackled directly. It requires focus and specific training in order to control the damages of a primitive neural system out of control. A religious Jew must engage in a daily internal battle between the primitive and advanced neural systems just as any Jew engages in battle between the positive and negative inclinations (*yetzer tov* and *yetzer hara*). A truly religious person should not come to believe that the behavior of others is a threat to his or her survival since this represents a lack of true faith.

Conclusion

The battle to overcome hatred has two distinct aspects: prevention and repair. In this chapter we proposed the following methods to prevent new episodes of hatred: (1) we must understand that the relationships most likely to produce hate triggers can be grouped into a "personal map" including siblings, parents, cousins, in-laws, colleagues in the workplace, and neighbors; (2) when we interact with those individuals, we must learn to employ our higher analytical capabilities to immediately distinguish between an unpleasant interaction (a joke, a tease, an embarrassment) and a threat, because we know that our primitive neural system feeds on our insecurities and mislabels any unpleasant interaction as a threat, triggering a disproportionate response; (3) when an interaction is hurtful, we should refrain from considering ourselves as "victims" and take the initiative to speak to the "aggressor" in a respectful, non-accusatory way and resolve the issue as soon as possible, keeping in mind that it is insignificant in the large scheme of life's problems; (4) if we do not, we end up traveling with an enormous load of "carry-on" luggage; (5) we must understand the challenges of the broader hatred map in the Diaspora and in Israel, particularly the dangers of prejudice and stereotypes associated with differences in political views, ethnicity, and degree of apparent religiosity.

10

How to Repair Existing Episodes of Baseless Hatred

The previous chapter described the first phase of the implementation plan for the proposed new paradigm to build *arevut* and make the Jewish people a moral nation. The methods focused on prevention of new episodes of baseless hatred. This chapter addresses the second part of the plan: how to repair existing relationships that have been ruined by hatred. We will also discuss how to reach the "next level," i.e., the self-transformation needed to achieve a type of unity that is authentic.

In this section we are considering situations where hatred is a "fait accompli," where an average Jew already feels hatred toward another Jew based on a previous incident. In the situations considered, it is assumed that the hater did not speak to the victim about the incident or that any discussion did not resolve the incident. Since that time, the hater left the hate unattended. We also assume that the hater acknowledges harboring a desire for revenge and retaliation. What can we advise the hater? Where does the hater draw the strength needed to forgive a perceived insult or injury that feels like a wound? What method should the hater use to get rid of the simmering hate?

There is no known cure for hate and there is no failsafe approach to uprooting hate. The proposed method rests on exposing the hater to the consequences and irrational aspects of his or her hate. The method fights hatred through awareness, understanding, and wisdom. Through his or her wisdom, the hater becomes able to create an emotional shift away from hate. It becomes obvious that nursing hatred indefinitely is absurd, foolish, and hurtful to the hater. The process that leads to such an awareness and emotional shift takes time but is achievable. When the inner work is complete, the hater can decide whether or how to approach the victim of hate.

Awareness of Consequences of Hatred

Hate Is Not Just Your Private Affair

Scenario 10.1: The Business Partner

Yossi went into business with his brother-in-law Yonatan. The partnership did not go well. Yossi left the business angry and Yonatan kept running the business. When some family members speak to Yossi to make peace between them, Yossi refuses and claims: "I treated him as a brother-in-law and acted in good faith; I loaned him money and he cheated me; he used my money and made deals without me. My hatred is my private affair and no one else's business!"

This is what the family members should have told Yossi to help him realize the consequences of his hatred: Although the events that led to your feelings are "personal" and this situation is emotionally consuming, you (Yossi) should not make the mistake of thinking that the issue is a private affair. When you hate Yonatan, you transform him into an enemy, and you do so for a long time. In your mind, you made him your hostage, but in reality you are the hostage. Yonatan belongs to his family and to the Jewish people and all of us have a stake in him. When you hate your brother-in-law, you exclude him from your world and exclude yourself from his world (as explained in chapter 4). So you have destroyed the bridge that connected him to you and nullified the covenant of *arevut* that is supposed to unite all of us. Your hatred created a hole in our family and our "national boat" and it makes us all sink!

The same applies to any hatred aimed at a member of the personal map.

In scenario 9.1, one week after the death of their mother, Naftali and his sister Nehama ended their sibling relationship. We, the Jewish people, should not remain indifferent to this ruined relationship, and we could address Naftali, saying: "We expected you, Naftali, the older brother, to look after your sister because both of you just became orphans. Instead, both of you were swallowed up by hatred. Was that jewelry worth that much? Or is it because your ego is more important than your brotherly duties? One concrete result is that your extended family is no longer whole and we, the Jewish people, have one more hole in our boat."

In scenario 9.2.1, we could address Ari as follows: Ari, you cannot accept that your sister Hannah is happy with her husband Ofir. At their wedding, both families (Hannah's and Ofir's) expected a happy relationship and not to become disunited. Similarly, in scenario 9.2.2, the family of your wife Malka did not expect tension during family gatherings just because you might be jealous of Tzvi's wealth at his young age. Suppose that you are correct and that your in-laws spoiled their children. How does that justify your intolerance of Tzvi? In the relationships with both brothers in-law, you seem to be the problem. We, the Jewish people, expected you to act as a bridge to both sides of your family; instead you created two more holes in the Jewish boat.

It should be evident by now that every episode of hatred has broad ramifications. That may seem like an exaggeration, but an example was given at the end of chapter 3 in connection with the destruction of Jerusalem and the Second Temple, and the subsequent exile. One would expect that such cataclysmic national tragedies would be caused by events of a grand, surreal nature. Yet the sages took us to a private party where a messenger had simply confused similar names of two guests.[1] The problem was that one of them was viewed as an enemy by the host. When that enemy-guest was about to be ejected, he hoped that the sages would not consider this scene "a private affair" but would intervene and save him. When they did not, he targeted everyone.

Hatred appears to be a private emotional affair but it is not. It can have large ripple effects. As explained in chapters 3 and 4, it spreads, violates the commitment of mutual responsibility, and tears down the unity of the Jewish people.

You Are Entitled to Justice, Not Revenge

In scenario 10.1, we can appeal to Yossi's reason as follows: You feel justified in hating because you are victim of an injustice. Assuming that your perception withstands legal examination, you are entitled to seek reparation. Therefore, your focus should be on recuperating the amount owed to you, not on revenge or wishing that Yonatan ends up in a car crash or that he acquires an incurable disease (as we heard you say). Once you recuperate your money, what would be your reason for not moving to the next step and forgiving?

---

1 Kaplan, *The Story of Tisha B'Av*, 19.

Hatred Damages Your Victim

Continuing with scenario 10.1: Yossi, you do not wish Yonatan well. You rejoice when you hear negative reports about him and you avoid opportunities to hear anything positive about him. It is well known that a hater chooses to remain ignorant in order to avoid weakening his hate, because deep down, the hater seeks the annihilation of the object of hate. If your negative feelings spread to anyone else in your circle, Yonatan will become isolated and his reputation affected. Ask yourself: What is the reason to perpetuate this state of affairs? How does that benefit you? Or anyone?

Hatred Makes You Participate in Gossip

Continuing with scenario 10.1: Yossi, you did not notice the following: when you harbored these hurtful feelings toward Yonatan, you devalued and dehumanized him. In your mind, he practically became a "non-human" and as such, became not entitled to your empathy. This is why you find it easy to speak negatively about anything he does and you experience a perverse pleasure in hearing negative reports about him.

Hatred Damages You

Continuing with scenario 10.1: Yossi, as soon as you became a hater, you were altered. Hatred not only destroys empathy but it engenders perverse empathy, meaning delight in the suffering of one's enemy. Therefore, whether or not you admit it, hatred has turned you into a cruel person. In addition, hatred warped your thinking because the primitive neural system does not just enslave a person: it fuses hate with meaning and justification. It made you obsessed, unproductive, and potentially depressed and self-destructive.

You can undo all the damage hatred did to you with one look or one smile!

The Person You Hate Is Both Despicable and Important to You

As a general principle, we are hurt by someone's words only if that person is meaningful to us. For example, when we tour a foreign country and someone in a marketplace screams at us, we do not hold a grudge and we forget about it after returning home. That is not the case when we have been hurt by a member of the personal hatred map: we do not forget the incident as easily. Although we refuse to admit it, the reason we are hurt is that, deep down, we consider that person important, a "peer" (or *ahikha*, "your brother"). Thus as a hater, you end up with a paradoxical attitude: the person you hate is both important and despicable! That realization can help, if you are willing to be honest and accept that this person is in fact important to you.

This dilemma is particularly visible when hatred erupts between siblings. In that case, the hater is torn: on one hand, he or she does not wish well to that sibling; on the other, he or she experiences feelings of pain and guilt when that sibling suffers a life tragedy. Tragically, there are many occurrences of siblings who are not on speaking terms and who meet at the funeral of their parents. That type of situation creates inner stress that gnaws at the hater and is dangerous to his or her health.

Awareness of Irrational Aspects of Hatred

You Turned from "Victim" to Aggressor

In scenario 1.1, Shimon said to Reuven: "Reuven, you must be hungry!" According to Reuven, he was the "victim" while Shimon was the "aggressor." But that assessment was made during the incident and was based on Reuven's perspective. Later, when Reuven reacted by hating Shimon, Shimon became the victim of hate. What can we say to Reuven? Hatred feels so natural that you, Reuven, have difficulty accepting that you turned from victim to long-term aggressor. The feeling of victimization provides you consolation, meaning, and justification, and blinds you. Once you take responsibility for your hatred and recognize that you are no longer a victim but an aggressor, the next step is to become uncomfortable with the status of aggressor and the associated unfair and damaging consequences. At that point, you are at a starting point for recovery.

Your Hatred Abstracted Only One Snapshot of a Whole Relationship

When you hate a family member or a friend, you should not view the incident or the insult in a vacuum but in the context of the whole relationship with that person over time. If you ever received some benefit from that family member, you are also bound by the responsibility of gratitude (*hakarat hatov*). Jews attach unique special significance to gratitude for numerous fundamental and historical reasons. Let us apply this reasoning to scenario 1.2, in which Sarah kept a grudge against her mother-in-law because she felt insulted by a comment about her wedding dress. Even if Sarah was very hurt, she must also accept that her mother-in-law sacrificed to raise her husband, Avi, and help him achieve his professional status. Sarah still benefits on a daily basis from her mother-in-law's efforts. Therefore she cannot dismiss them and she owes her mother-in-law gratitude. If Sarah is honest, this should help convince her to begin traveling the path of forgiveness.

Your Expectation of Respect and Honor Is a Trap

In our interactions with members of the personal hatred map, we react rapidly and sometimes harshly when we are not given the honor we feel we deserve. Most of us do not realize that others can only treat us according to their own criteria and will not shower us with honor according to our expectations. Another complexity comes from the fact that the less we respect someone, the more we expect that person to give us honor. That is a dangerous trap and a dead end because it is not possible to extract honor from others. Trying to do so only leads to failure and disappointment.

The path of wisdom dictates that it is more fruitful to work on freeing ourselves from the addiction to recognition and honor. By building our self-confidence, we lower our expectations and become less subject to disappointments since anyway, others cannot meet our expectations. Therefore, if you are in a hatred episode caused by bruised honor, you should be willing to forgive because there is chronically a gap between your expectations and what others can provide.

Hatred Does Not Solve Problems

A hater generally believes that hatred is an appropriate response because it was made in "self-defense," in reaction to a perceived affront. For example, when you as a hater have an encounter with the person you hate, you make a point not to say hello, and you feel good, thinking, "I am ignoring him; he does not deserve my acknowledgment!" The reality is that those hatred feelings serve no purpose and solve nothing for you. On the contrary, they only serve to isolate and alienate you.

Are You Selfish Enough to Forgive?

This is suggested as the last reason to forgive because it appeals to your selfishness. Assuming that, as a hater, you feel no inclination to forgive the perceived insult based on the above reasons, there is a rationale to forgive based on the following reasoning: Your hate does not diminish on its own; as long as you hate and keep a grudge, you remain obsessed by the person you hate and you are practically imprisoned by that person! Therefore, make the effort to forgive just so that you can free yourself from that obsession and from being a hostage.

Even though this approach is not altruistic, it can be a starting point because the hater will eventually realize the truth: I was trapped because of my insecurities and my dependence on others. When I forgive, I become self-reliant, I free myself, and I cure myself from a disease.

The Next Level: Empathy

Until now, we have been concerned with methods to avoid and repair the hurtful and damaging effects of hatred, appealing to a person's wisdom and rational mind. Another approach to overcome the strong emotional pull of hatred is to generate the antidote emotion: empathy. The acquisition of empathy effectuates a self-transformation that restores the bond of *arevut* that connects Jews and turns them into caring and supportive individuals.

What Is Empathy?

Empathy has been defined by scientists as "a vicarious experience of others' emotions"[2] or "a binding force among persons."[3] It is the capability of one person to share another person's feelings – their joy or their pain. In everyday language, it is referred to as the ability to "put oneself in someone else's shoes." It is different from sympathy; we have sympathy for our friends, whereas empathy is the capacity of feeling for someone for whom we may have little sympathy.

Empathy and Hatred

Empathy is closely related to hatred. Already in the general background on generic hatred (chapter 1), we learned that hatred suppresses the potential for empathy toward others; whatever emotional affinity we have toward others disappears when hatred is allowed to take hold. The

---

2   Spinella, "Prefrontal Substrates," 175–81.

3   Paul J. Eslinger, "Neurological and Neuropsychological Bases of Empathy," *European Neurology* 39, no. 4 (1998): 193–99.

mutually exclusive nature of hatred and empathy provides an answer to the often-asked question: How can soldiers remain blind to the suffering of civilian victims during genocides? How do they lose their "normal" humanity? Answer: their hatred "protects" them from having any emotion; with hatred as a cover, they become able to torture their prisoners, behave in the cruelest fashion, and yet feel no remorse. That is the "power" – or more appropriately the danger – of hatred as a destroyer of human empathy.

Empathy: An Advanced Capacity

Basic empathy is a potential, a capability that can be developed. It has been described as "one of the mind's most advanced capacities."[4] It is called an advanced capacity because it allows us to experience emotions in a variety of situations. It allows us to reexperience a previous emotion like an embarrassment in public. Amazingly, it allows us to experience even hypothetical emotions, emotions that we would feel under imagined situations. In addition to this high level of emotional thinking for ourselves, it allows us to comprehend other people's inner experiences, literally to penetrate their internal frames of reference. That is how the capacity of empathy allows us to identify with others and build bridges with their emotional data banks.

Studies in patients with cerebral damage have shown that anatomically, empathy belongs in one of the most advanced areas of the human brain (the orbitofrontal cortex and associated networks)[5]. However, when the primitive neural system is in control, it decreases the capacity for empathy to the point of disabling it. To develop empathy, we must engage in a chronic battle between both neural systems and ascertain that the advanced one remains dominant. That requires education, training, and challenging our beliefs.

---

4 Dozier, *Why We Hate*, 231.

5 Eslinger, "Bases of Empathy," 193–99.

Developing Empathy

The training includes a number of steps: first adopting and remaining focused on an "us-us" perspective, and systematically rejecting the "us-them" dichotomy. To do so, the first step is to recognize the links between stereotype, prejudice, and eventually, hate. The process is neatly described by Chris Frith:

> We are innately predisposed to be prejudiced. All our social interactions begin with prejudice. The content of these prejudices has been acquired through our interactions with friends and acquaintances and through hearsay.... Our prejudices begin with stereotypes.... Social stereotypes provide the starting point for our interactions with people we don't know. They enable us to make our initial guesses about the person's intentions.... The guesses and predictions we make from this limited knowledge will not be very good.[6]

Our primitive neural system is very adept at binary and negative stereotyping. Because it operates in generalizations, it separates between our group and the other, resulting in a clear "us" versus "them" distinction. Prejudice comes in under normal circumstances because we value our group more highly or because the other is viewed negatively for any reason: dress, skin color, language, neighborhood, etc. It works by characterizing a whole group by one trait – more often than not negative. This "us" versus "them" type of thinking is widespread and occurs commonly in everyday life. As mentioned above, most everyone carries stereotypes based on lack of knowledge, first impressions, appearances, hearsay, gossip, headlines, and generalizations.

A more proactive approach to developing empathy is to exercise one's will and act in a fashion that enhances caring for others. This is based

---

6 Frith, *Making Up the Mind*, 167–68.

on an original approach about the inner mechanics of love of others taught by Rabbi E. Dessler. He asks the following question about the exact relationship between love and giving: "Is giving a consequence of love or is love a result of giving?" Intuitively, it seems that giving is a consequence of love since we give gifts to people we love. His answer is the counterintuitive opposite: "We love those to whom we give," for the following reason: giving to a person creates love for that person for the same reason that people feel attached to anything that they have created. The rationale is that the giver recognizes a part of himself or herself in the object created or in the person to whom he or she gave. The underlying principle is that we are attached to the work of our hands because of our love of ourselves – a love we can always count on.

This principle has numerous consequences: if we want to connect with others and find a part of ourselves in them, all we have to do is give to them. Here we mean material gifts but also the gifts of acceptance and tolerance. The willingness to take those concrete steps trains our advanced neural system in developing empathy for others. As a result, we begin to identify with them and their feelings; we respect their human dignity; we are careful not to embarrass them or hurt them; we look out for their welfare. Most importantly, it becomes more difficult to stereotype them, to devalue and dehumanize them, and therefore to hate them. Also, through developing empathy for others we become more capable of resolving differences and conflicts and ultimately of forgiving if hatred has developed. Forgiving can be done privately (in one's heart) but restoring a damaged relationship is considered a heroic act. It should be obvious that this approach is applicable and useful in relationships between spouses.

Empathy for Jews

In chapter 5 and in this chapter we suggested reasons why interactions between Jews might be difficult, such as intolerance of each other's opinion and the so-called "last Jew" syndrome.

The strong individuality of Jews can be related to the three terms used to designate a Jew: *Ivri*, *Yisrael*, and *Yehudi*. The first term, *Ivri*, referred first to Abraham,[7] *Yisrael* refers to Jacob,[8] and *Yehudi* refers to Mordechai, hero of the Purim story.[9] All of them reflect the trait of individuality and determination to take a moral stance as manifested by Abraham, Jacob, and Yehudah in the stories of their lives (not described here). We should admit that individuality is fostered by the educational approach: in a traditional Jewish educational framework, children are always taught to ask important questions. Individuality is an expression of inner strength. Were it not for that strength, how would the Jews have survived until now?

The price of strong individuality is twofold: it makes an individual less tolerant and it makes that same person difficult to tolerate. We should be willing to pay that price in Jewish society since, as we indicated, intolerance might be based on caring. Why not learn to tolerate differences in opinion, since questioning has been part of our tradition? For example, on what grounds do we appropriate the right to decide whether another person's style of Jewishness is inappropriate? In most instances, that "right" is presumptuous, because we never have enough information on the other to decide whether that person is unwilling or simply unable to meet our expectations (assuming that our expectations represent valid national or halachic standards). Our individual right to be Jewish was a gift, inherited at birth (or acquired upon halakhic

---

7 See Genesis 14:13 for Abraham. The term was also used to designate Joseph, the Jewish midwives, and Moses as a baby.

8 See Genesis 32:29, when Jacob's name was changed by the angel.

9 Megillat Esther 2:5.

conversion). Empathy addresses these issues because it enables and facilitates tolerance of others at multiple levels.

Why do we feel so threatened by the political or religious positions of other Jews? Why do we react more to those positions than to the views of our collective enemies, whether in Israel or in the Diaspora? We do not have to be threatened by the fact that each Jew takes individual responsibility for the survival of the whole Jewish people ("last Jew" syndrome). We make the choice to be threatened by it; we can instead decide to appreciate it. Why not distinguish between being against people and being against their attitudes or judgments? Even if a particular Jew has very different values that are truly not acceptable, why not treat him or her as a stranger? Jewish tradition dictates that we love the stranger and treat him or her with care.[10] Our tradition warns most about the widow, the orphan, and the stranger, because they are vulnerable. So let us treat the Jew we do not like as a stranger. Alternatively, we should be like parents: they have empathy toward their children in spite of their character defects.

A separate reason to develop empathy toward Jews deals with elimination of intra-Jewish stereotypes for purely historical reasons, i.e., because Jews have suffered so much from stereotyping at the hand of their enemies. The danger of stereotyping and prejudice is that they group people in such a way that they are no longer individuals; then it becomes easy to lose objectivity and any feeling toward them disappears. This technique was used extensively by the Nazis: first they produced the group category of race in which their race (Aryan) was superior. Then, they marginalized Jews, then devalued them, then dehumanized them, then equated them with vermin, then used them as scapegoats for the

---

10 Amsel, *Jewish Encyclopedia*, 220. There he provides several sources specifying how careful Jews must be about the treatment of strangers.

poor economy, then as scapegoats for the war, then they became the enemy within; finally, genocide becomes the only solution to solve the country's problems.

Parenthetically, this is why displays in Holocaust museums always begin with the campaigns that were waged to marginalize and dehumanize Jews several years before the war and the genocide. Even today, the external hatred faced by Israel (described in chapters 6 and 7) relies on the same techniques of promoting stereotypes and prejudice. For these historical reasons, Jews have a moral obligation to banish all prejudice against other Jews. Also, as mentioned before, since Jews are still hated today, why should we not protect them from our own hatred and that of other Jews? Jews need support, not additional hatred that has no basis!

But all this cannot take place if we do not remove the main barrier to empathy that exists within ourselves: it is the "space" occupied by our ego. To have empathy, we must make room for others within ourselves. The room for the other is not next to us, it is inside of us. That room can only come at the expense of the space occupied by our ego. One benefit of that exercise is that a diminished ego leads to personal contentment and happiness.

Summary

This chapter addressed the challenges of repairing existing relationships that have been destroyed by hatred. The proposed approach rests on the value of becoming aware of the consequences and irrational aspects of hatred. With that awareness, any person with average wisdom is likely to be moved toward forgiveness (even if the object of hate is not approached).

The following consequences of hatred were discussed:

1. Hatred is not just your private affair.

2. You are entitled to justice, not revenge.

3. Hatred damages the person you hate.

4. Hatred makes you participate in gossip, as an author and recipient.

5. Hatred damages you.

6. The person you hate seems despicable, yet that person is important to you.

The following irrational aspects of hatred were outlined:

1. You feel like a victim, yet you are the aggressor.

2. Your hatred focuses on only one instant of a whole relationship.

3. Your overinflated ego makes you expect respect and honor, but extracting honor from others is not achievable.

4. You are under the illusion that your hatred serves you, but it does not solve any problem.

5. If you are rational, you should use your selfishness to forgive.

To enhance the chances of success of these steps, the hater must overcome the strong emotional pull and comfort provided by hatred. To achieve that objective, we proposed developing empathy, which functions as the antidote to hatred. In chapter 2's discussion about hate and love, we pointed out that the commandment against hatred was followed by "You shall love your neighbor as yourself." Almost everyone smiles when it is brought up because they know that practically, it has remained an ideal. The development of empathy, as outlined above, represents a concrete step to achieving that lofty goal. By allowing a connection to the humanity and uniqueness of others, empathy allows us to rebuild our national fabric and become a moral society.

Afterword

Hatred affects all humans but baseless hatred is lethal to Jews because it dissolves away their unity. It transforms the Jewish people into a "mixed multitude."[1] At this point in time, because we come late in Jewish history, we have a clearer picture of the dangers of baseless hatred than the Jews had in 70 CE, when it became a fatal entity. Through the long exile that followed, we have seen that the consequences of baseless hatred can be serious because Jews are always subjected to the hatred of antisemitism, old or modern.

More than once, baseless hatred has brought the Jewish people to the brink of destruction. But what have we done about it? Some Jews dedicate one out of 365 days each year (the Ninth of Av) or the three preceding weeks to remember it. Others also mourn between the holidays of Pessah and Shavuot. More can and must be done to curb baseless hatred now, based on the emergence of the first Jewish society in nineteen centuries, the State of Israel.

The analysis of baseless hatred presented in the previous chapters suggests that baseless hatred has persisted because the phenomenon of hatred and its consequences are not understood. Baseless hatred is not recognized for what it is: a lethal disease. We have come to accept hatred as inevitable even though we see that it is cruel and destroys the unity and peace of our families. Who can honestly claim that his or her family is not affected? The prevalence is global: hatred behaves as a fire that cannot be extinguished, as a contagious infectious disease that spreads out of control. Hatred destroys the personality of the hater, who becomes

---

1   In the Hebrew language, this is a play on words: a mixed multitude is called *erev rav*; hatred transforms the Jewish people from *arevim* (mutually responsible) to *erev rav* (mixed multitude).

vindictive, revengeful, diminished, and abnormal. But, unfortunately, all these transformations are not visible. Presenting with an apparently normal behavior, the hater is infected by a form of temporary insanity which is conveniently not recognized but is treatable. How long will we remain silent while we witness our brothers and sisters consumed by the mental pain and anguish of hatred that lasts for whole lifetimes?

The first step in curbing hatred is to bring it out in the open, to recognize it and to point to it without being ashamed. These steps have worked in the campaigns against gossip,[2] and we now see men and women who refuse to hear gossip and have become able to speak without maligning others. That recent success is admirable and encouraging. Recognizing a disease for what it is has also been successful in tackling many medical and social problems (the AIDS epidemic, sexual abuse of children). If we take simple steps as individuals, within our small circles of family, friends, and neighbors, the epidemic of hate and its consequences will be greatly diminished.

At this juncture in Jewish history, we have even more at stake: we must preserve the integrity of the only Jewish society, the State of Israel. Wherever Jews may reside in the world, their future is being played out in the Land of Israel. We cannot allow the scourge of hatred to "dissolve" the fabric of the Jewish people. We cannot take the risk of reversing the gains of nineteen centuries. In the field of hate, we can make enormous gains simply by working within our own families and circles of influence.

The second step would be to improve the formal teaching of baseless hatred in the curricula of Jewish schools everywhere. To address the future of the Jewish people in a serious way, there is an urgent need to assist the new generation of Jews in its self-transformation by creating

2 Chofetz Chaim Heritage Foundation worldwide Shmiras Haloshon initiative.

in-depth teaching materials on the different aspects of baseless hatred. The human brain exhibits unexpected plasticity at a young age and gets programmed in ways that affect adult behavior. Between the ages of five and seven, children become able to separate categories, grasp hierarchies, and begin to understand who should or should not be trusted.

It is known that the effects of the environment are critical: just as children who grow up in an environment of hatred and vengeance absorb it easily (chapter 6), "young children who have been removed from a prejudiced environment and grow up in a non-prejudiced environment will tend to have a significantly less biased outlook than their peers who remain behind."[3] This is the case even when those "removed children" are under the influence of parents and family members who kept their prejudices: "By the third generation, these prejudices may have completely disappeared."[4]

It should be simple enough to develop educational resources and classroom materials including the distinction between generic hatred and baseless hatred, the history and significance of *arevut*, and its cementing role in the integrity of the Jewish people. An immediate starting point would be to teach teachers and parents. If parents begin to speak about baseless hatred at home, they will be compelled to become role models for their children and practice its principles in relationships with family, neighbors, and coworkers. That would be a substantial achievement and a legacy from the present generation.

Jews are not alone when it comes to hatred. The whole world is already affected by the phenomenon of hatred, considered by many to be one of the world's most pressing issues. Just in the last few decades, it has been shown that hatred can cause wars and genocides based on religion, race,

---

3 Dozier, *Why We Hate*, 248.

4 Ibid.

or simply politics, as pointed out by several world experts:

"Hate is the nuclear weapon of the mind. Its detonation can blow apart the social order and plunge nations into war and genocide."[5]

"This may be humanity's last chance to solve this daunting problem."[6]

As a first step toward achieving *arevut* and unity, Jews should unite in recognizing hatred as a lethal disease. The task of conquering it may be daunting, but its time has come. We, the Jews, are uniquely sensitive and qualified to address it. It may be our next major contribution to humankind.

---

5 Ibid., 1.

6 Ibid., 30.

Bibliography

Amsel, Nachum. *The Jewish Encyclopedia of Moral and Ethical Issues*. Northvale, NJ: Jason Aronson, 1994.

Bard, Mitchell G. *Myths and Facts: A Guide to the Arab-Israeli Conflict*. Chevy Chase, MD: American Israeli Cooperative Enterprise, 2006.

Baumeister, Roy F., and David A. Butz. "Roots of Hate, Violence, and Evil." Chapter 5 in *The Psychology of Hate*, edited by Robert J. Sternberg. Washington, DC: American Psychological Association, 2005.

Beilin, Yossi. *Israel: A Concise Political History*. New York: St. Martin's, 1992.

Ben-Gurion, David. *Memoirs*. Cleveland: The World Publishing Company, 1970.

Berman, Paul. *The Flight of the Intellectuals*. Brooklyn: Melville House, 2010.

Chertoff, Mordecai S., ed. *Zionism: A Basic Reader*. New York: Herzl Press, 1975.

Ciechanover, Aaron. Letter to the editor. *Azure* 31 (2008).

Dolan, R.J. "The Human Amygdala and Orbital Prefrontal Cortex in Behavioural Regulation." In *Mental Processes in the Human Brain*, edited by Jon Driver et al., 49–68. New York: Oxford University Press, 2008.

Dozier, Rush W., Jr. *Why We Hate: Understanding, Curbing, and Eliminating Hate in Ourselves and Our World*. New York: McGraw-Hill, 2002.

Driver, Jon, et al., ed. *Mental Processes in the Human Brain*. New York: Oxford University Press, 2008.

Eslinger, Paul J. "Neurological and Neuropsychological Bases of Empathy." *European Neurology* 39, no. 4 (1998): 193–99.

Fallaci, Oriana. "Sull'antisemitismo" [On antisemitism]. Panorama, April 18, 2002. Translated from the original Italian by David A. Harris, in *In the Trenches: Selected Speeches and Writings of an American Jewish Activist*, vol. 3, 2002–2003. Jersey City, NJ: Ktav, 2004.

Finkielkraut, Alain. "The Religion of Humanity and the Sin of the Jews." *Azure* 21 (2005): 23.

Frith, Chris. *Making Up the Mind: How the Brain Creates Our Mental World*. Malden, MA: Blackwell Publishing, 2007.

Fromkin, David. *A Peace to End All Peace: The Fall of the Ottoman Empire and the Creation of the Modern Middle East*. New York: Henry Holt and Company, 1989.

Gaarder, Jostein. "God's Chosen People." *Aftenposten*, August 5, 2006.

Glick, Caroline B. *Shackled Warrior: Israel and the Global Jihad*. Jerusalem: Gefen Publishing House, 2008.

Gold, Dore. "The Challenge to Israel's Legitimacy." In *Israel at 60*. Jerusalem Center for Public Affairs, 2009.

Gordis, Daniel. *Saving Israel: How the Jewish People Can Win a War That May Never End*. Hoboken, NJ: Wiley, 2009.

Halevi, Rabbi Pinhas of Barcelona. *Sefer haHinnuch: Student Edition*, translated by Charles Wengrov. Jerusalem: Feldheim Publishers, 1992.

Harris, David A. *In the Trenches: Selected Speeches and Writings of an American Jewish Activist*. Vol. 3, 2002–2003. Jersey City, NJ: Ktav, 2004.

Hazony, Yoram. "Judaism and the Modern State." *Azure* 21 (2005): 33.

Horowitz, Edward. *How the Hebrew Language Grew*. Jersey City, NJ: Ktav, 1960.

Kagan, Israel Meir haCohen. *Sefer Chafetz Chayim*. Translated by Yedidya Levy. New York: Mazal Press, 2004.

Kaplan, Aryeh. *Jerusalem: The Eye of the Universe*. New York: NCSY/UOJC, 1976.

———. "The Omer." In *Seasons of the Soul: Religious, Historical, and Philosophical Perspectives on the Jewish Year and Its Milestones*, edited by Rabbi Nisson Wolpin, 224–229. New York: Mesorah Publications, 1981.

Lévy, Bernard-Henri. "Why I Defend Israel." *The Huffington Post*, June 7, 2010.

Luzzatto, Moshe Chaim. *Orchot Tzaddikim: The Ways of the Tzaddikim*. Nanuet, NY: Feldheim Publishers, 1995.

Morris, Benny. *One State, Two States: Resolving the Israel/Palestine Conflict*. New Haven: Yale University Press, 2009.

Nasr, Vali. *The Shia Revival: How Conflicts within Islam Will Shape the Future*. New York: W.W. Norton, 2006.

Pear, Ian. *The Accidental Zionist: What a Priest, a Pornographer and a Wrestler Named Chainsaw Taught Me about Being Jewish, Saving the World and Why Israel Matters to Both*. Jerusalem: New Song Publishers, 2008.

Peres, Shimon, with Arye Naor. *The New Middle East*. New York: Henry Holt and Company, 1993.

Prager, Dennis. "An Open Letter to Israel's Jews." *Jewish Journal*, June 15, 2010.

Rosenthal, Donna. *The Israelis: Ordinary People in an Extraordinary Land*. New York: Free Press, 2003.

Sacks, Jonathan. *Future Tense: Jews, Judaism, and Israel in the Twenty-First Century*. New York: Schocken, 2009.

———. *One People? Tradition, Modernity, and Jewish Unity*. Portland, OR: The Littman Library of Jewish Civilization, 1993.

Sharansky, Natan. "On Hating the Jews." *Commentary* 116 (November 2003): 26–34.

———. "The Political Legacy of Theodor Herzl." *Azure* 21 (2005): 87.

Shlaim, Avi. *War and Peace in the Middle East: A Concise History*. New York: Penguin, 1994.

Spinella, Marcello. "Prefrontal Substrates of Empathy: Psychometric Evidence in a Community Sample." *Biological Psychiatry* 70, no. 3 (December 2005): 175–81.

Steele, Shelby. "Israel and the Surrender of the West." *Wall Street Journal*, June 21, 2010.

Sternberg, Robert J., ed. *The Psychology of Hate*. Washington, DC: American Psychological Association, 2005.

———, and Karin Sternberg. *The Nature of Hate*. New York: Cambridge University Press, 2008.

Suissa, David. "In Praise of Disunity." *Jewish Journal*, June 15, 2010.

Wiesel, Elie. "We Choose Honor." *Parade*, October 28, 2001, 4–5.

Made in the USA
Columbia, SC
02 March 2021